LAYING THE FOUND— ATIONS

Author and designer: Andrew Couldwell

Editor: Meagan Fisher Couldwell

CON— TENTS

VIII

FOREWORD

Meagan Fisher Couldwell

10

INTRODUCTION

Real talk

Who is this book for?

The role of development in design

Technology moves too fast for print

System design is not a scary thing

Systematic design

This book will help you and your team

20

**CHAPTER 1:
WHAT IS A DESIGN SYSTEM?**

Why are design systems important?

When do we need design systems?

Leading the way

26

**CHAPTER 2:
SELLING A DESIGN SYSTEM**

Find your partners

Laying the foundations

Start small, and adjust your pitch
accordingly

At what stage do you sell?

The importance and quality of 'the sell'

A word on office politics

38

CHAPTER 3:
LAYING THE FOUNDATIONS

Putting up scaffolding

The importance of brand in system design

Marketing vs. product

Digital Foundations

— Mission, values, and principles

— Brand identity

— Brand tone of voice and copywriting

— Formatting

— Accessibility and inclusivity

— Responsive design

— Process

— Design systems

How are brand guidelines different to design system documentation?

Make it visible, make it count

Just get it done!

Flaunt it

Don't lose sight of why you're doing this...

80

CHAPTER 4:
DESIGN SYSTEM MODEL

Speaking the same language

The Foundations Model

Foundations

Components

Patterns

Templates and Pages

Design systems in product design

A case study of a design system at work

Allow for flexibility

106

CHAPTER 5:
GETTING STARTED

Start by identifying the problems

Where do we go from here?

Be smart about which approach you choose

114

CHAPTER 6:
AN ITERATIVE APPROACH

Find your team

Interface audits

Colour audits

Code audits

Visual audits

What now?

Managing the workload

The Frankenstein monster effect

Refinement vs. exploration

128

CHAPTER 7:
A WHOLESALE APPROACH

Design exploration

Ground your work in reality

Building a visual language

Build and launch plans

It doesn't have to be perfect

Wholesale design, and an iterative build
and launch

The disruption factor

Rolling out a design system, responsibly

140

CHAPTER 8:
SYSTEMATISING THE DESIGN

Set the system up for success

You need a design system library

Constraints are not a bad thing

Tools for the job

Naming conventions

Colour system

Guidelines for colour

Limited text styles

Editable components

Cover all states of components

Pattern library

Design tokens and Sass variables

Designer access to code

Tracking and organising system tasks

180

CHAPTER 9:
DOCUMENT EVERYTHING!

More than a style guide

The basics

Better together

Don't leave documentation until last

Document as you go

What should you document?

— Do's and don'ts

— Colour

— Brand identity

— Typography

— Copywriting

— Components

— Patterns

— Don't forget the small things

— Grid, layout, and spacing

— Design tokens

How do you document a design system?

Getting started, the easy way

Living style guides

If not a Google Doc, then what?

220

CHAPTER 10:
GALLERY

Inspirational examples of great
documentation

242

CHAPTER 11:
MAINTAINING A DESIGN SYSTEM

Work with shared design assets

Working with patterns

Keep documentation up to date

Keeping the design and code in sync

Code as a design tool

Keep your team in the loop

Guardians, ambassadors, and leaders

Closing thoughts

260

THE AUTHOR

Andrew Couldwell

Owl Studios

Club of the Waves

Acknowledgments

Dedication

LET'S GET STAR—TED

FORE—
WORD

— by Meagan Fisher Couldwell

@owltastic

There are many reasons why I'm so excited that you're holding this book right now. To start, Andrew has years of experience creating design systems for everyone from small, agile clients to big, complex teams — in fact, he was doing "system design" long before we had a name for it, and well before it first appeared in the growing list of skills which designers are required to know.

I, on the other hand, had long avoided thinking, reading, or talking about system design because it sounded big and terrifying and complicated. But conversations with Andrew about his approach made it feel simple, logical, and (believe it or not) fun to do. I've been telling him for years that he should write a book to help demystify system design for others, which is a big reason why I'm so glad this book is finally in your hands.

If you think system design won't work for your complicated team, or are confused by the jargon surrounding it, or just want to take some small steps today to be better at your job, this book is going to be a godsend for you. It's not written on behalf of any company, or to make anyone look good, so it's an honest and unflinching look at the challenges and rewards that come with designing systematically.

This book covers — and goes beyond — the more commonly explored topics surrounding how to create a design system. It also gives us a helpful framework for how we can work together to create better experiences, and shows us how to lower the barriers between different teams and roles.

In addition to drawing on his own 15+ years of experience as a web designer, product designer, developer, manager, and system design lead, this book includes a wealth of research; it covers case studies, articles, and examples from dozens of different teams.

Andrew often says "system design is really a term we use to talk about best design practices." The knowledge packed into this book will not only improve the way you create experiences, it will also empower you to build stronger teams and a better world. We can't wait to see what you do with it!

Meagan Caldwell

INTRO—
DUC—
TION

This book covers what design systems are, why they are important, and how to get stakeholder buy-in to create one. It introduces you to a simple model, and two very different approaches to creating a design system. What's unique about this book is its focus on the importance of brand in design systems, and creating documentation. It's a comprehensive, practical guide that's simple to follow and easy on the eye.

I've been designing and building websites, working on products, and creating design systems for over 15 years. During that time:

- I've been the solo designer and developer at a company.
- I've worked with small 1-5 person teams.
- I've worked with large 10-100+ person teams.
- I've led teams of designers.
- I've worked in-house, remotely, and as a freelancer.
- I've worked with and at small startups and large corporations.

I've seen things go so wrong, so many times. I've learned from those experiences, and worked with others to fix the problems we've encountered.

I've spent a lot of time learning, assimilating, and distilling all that I've learned down to its simplest form. I've sold the value of simple system design thinking, models, terminology, and values to designers, developers, and stakeholders.

After years of this, I'm left with dozens of Keynote decks, Google Docs, design systems docs, style guides, design files, code, scars, bruises, lessons learned, enemies, friends, and a head full of thoughts.

I decided to do something meaningful with all that experience. I sincerely hope you enjoy this book, and that it helps you and your team! :)

This is real talk about creating design systems. No jargon, no glossing over the hard realities, and no company hat. Just good advice, experience, and practical tips.

Real talk

Perhaps my "real talk" approach is because of my roots: I was born and raised in the industrious north of England, where people value hard work and plain speaking. Or perhaps it's all my experiences — good *and* bad — that have shaped the way I think and talk about designing and building websites and digital products.

I don't like jargon. I like to keep things simple. Nowhere is this more important than in system design, where communication and collaboration are essential. The simpler you keep things, the more successful you'll be. This is a theme throughout this book, from the design system model and terminology, to practical steps, to working with your team.

I could tell you how to design, build, and document a design system for yourself, as a personal project. It would be awesome, but I doubt that's a reality for many people reading this book. Chances are you work on, or lead a team at a company... Or you plan to.

The realities of working in-house at companies — especially large companies — are often very different from the rosy perspectives we read about on Medium and company blogs, and hear about in design talks. These stories are told by people wearing a company hat, who can only say generally positive things about their experience. They don't talk about office politics and other hard realities. I don't work for anyone but myself. I'll tell you — honestly — how to navigate the challenges of working in-house, with stakeholders, deadlines, legacy problems (design, code, and people!), and all the other *fun* challenges we encounter along the way.

I've been in the creative trenches, fighting for the designers and developers on my team, the brand, and the users. I've defeated the odds to create beautiful and meaningful work. It's not always easy. In fact, it's often very hard, and very tiring. Sometimes it even feels hopeless, but perseverance and the arsenal of knowledge you'll learn in this book will set you in good stead to create the best work of your career!

Who is this book for?

This book is definitely more design-focussed, but we'll be delving into the whole process — which involves much **more than just design.**

Selling, managing, and advocating are key to the success (or failure) of a design system. **You can design a system in a matter of days, but you won't get much**

further without the support and collaboration of developers, product managers, and other stakeholders. This book will help you reach and collaborate with these stakeholders.

We'll cover brand and digital guidelines, and how to create, document and roll out a design system. This book will also prepare you for how to build your team, and set your system up for success.

Building, integrating, and launching a design system is arguably the lion's share of the work. We won't be covering development processes or writing (much) code, but we'll certainly look at the overlap of design and development. It's important that design and engineering teams work together, which is a theme throughout this book.

The role of development in design

A design system will go nowhere without developers. A beautifully designed library of design components is useless if it lives only in design software and documentation. It has to be built, deployed, maintained, and scaled. Do you want to create a design system? **Developers are your new best friends** *(if they're not already, which they should be).*

Development should always be part of the design process. Designers and developers working in silo — or even physically separated from each other (in the workplace) — is bad for team culture, as well as the quality and efficiency of the work.

With any form of digital design — but especially system design — I encourage you to discard this (lazy) notion of 'the developers will figure it out'. Involve developers. Get them interested in building the system with you, not after you've finished designing it. We'll talk about this more throughout this book.

Technology moves too fast for print

This book intentionally avoids referencing specific tools or software, save for a few exceptions. Technology evolves so fast that anything I reference may be obsolete by the time you read this! *(Hello, it's 2018/19 as I write this).*

That said: the supporting website **(01)** for this book includes links to tools, resources, and articles relating to system design. They, at least, will remain current.

System design is not a scary thing

A good place to start is to discard this notion that system design is a scary process, or an exclusive club for the design elite. System design is nothing new. Unlike responsive design, Sass, CSS Grid, or Flexbox — nobody invented system design. It's just a term our industry has given to cover the processes and habits that lead to the most efficient digital design, development, and management. That's all.

Feel better? Good :)

Systematic design

It might be easier to view system design as 'a systematic approach to design'.

System design is about not tackling design problems in isolation, or as one-offs. It's about considering versatile solutions that can be used repeatedly and consistently throughout a product. It's about not creating a different way to solve the same or similar problem every time you come across it.

A design system is the end result of a systematic approach to design. It's the harmonious package of design, code, guidelines, and documentation that's used to build consistent, on-brand, and efficient websites and products.

The sobering reality

Here's the thing — and, sorry, this is the brutal and honest truth: if you're a designer working on websites, products or apps, and you're not designing (at least somewhat) systematically — you're doing more harm than good.

- Do you choose a different font, weight, or size for every header?
- Are you creating a different button every time you need a call to action?

Every time you design a different (unnecessary) solution, you're adding more complexity to the code. This leads to legacy problems. Future edits will be harder to make. Shipping new features or iterations will take longer. Page load times will increase. The user experience can be diminished. You get the picture.

01. designsystemfoundations.com

You're halfway there!

The good news is, you may already be designing systematically without even realising that's what you're doing.

- When you *decide* to use *only* two typefaces...
- When you use title case *instead of* sentence case *in certain scenarios*...
- When you *define* a set of text styles or pick a colour palette...
- When you design to a *consistent* grid or use *specific* spacing...

...and stick* to those design choices — you're designing systematically.

If you design systematically, you'll be a better digital designer for it. You don't necessarily have to create a design system, to 'do' system design! Not every project requires a design system. We'll get into this more throughout this book, but just keep in mind: even if you don't need a design system, don't currently have one, or your company won't grant you the time to create one, you should still take a systematic approach to design.

* To clarify: by "stick", I don't mean permanently. All design choices are subject to change and iteration.

This book will help you and your team

This book is about levelling up as a digital designer by taking those extra steps to go from designing systematically to creating a design system.

This book will help you formulate and document the design choices you and your team make. After all, a system wouldn't be much of a system without *rules*. Remember: the systematic design choices you make are no good just in your head — especially if you're working with a team.

We'll look at the importance of brand in system design — first by creating digital brand guidelines, then building design systems upon those solid foundations.

You'll learn about creating a design library of system elements that will enable your design team to work quickly, efficiently, and consistently.

I'll coach you on how to adjust your design system pitch to different stakeholders at your company in order to gain the support and momentum you need to succeed.

You can design a system in a matter of days, but you won't get much further without the support and collaboration of developers, product managers, and other stakeholders.

We'll talk (a lot) about the importance of finding your team, and working together to identify the problems in your product and processes — and practical things you can do to *fix* them. We'll even look at two different approaches to these problems: an 'iterative' approach, and a 'wholesale' approach.

And throughout this book, I'll share lots of real examples of design work, documentation, and best practices to illustrate the concepts covered.

Thank you for reading my book! I hope you enjoy it and find it useful. If you do like it, I'd really appreciate it if you'd recommend it to your friends, colleagues, and followers :)

— designsystemfoundations.com

@andrewcouldwell

WHAT IS A DESIGN SYS— TEM?

01

A design system is hard to summarise. It's perhaps easier to explain why design systems are important, and what they help us to do, than to explain exactly what they are. However, here's my attempt at a definition:

Design systems bring order and consistency to digital products. They help to protect the brand, elevate the user experience, and increase the speed and efficiency of how we design and build products. They are a source of truth and a system of record for our design decisions. They hold us to high standards, keep teams on the same page, and help to onboard new team members. They document the why, when, where, and how.

I should stress that the design, build, and 'rules' of a system are not set in stone — they are a constant work in progress, open to iteration to improve, adapt, and scale.

Designing and building on-brand, quality, and consistent digital products at scale is hard. It's even harder when your designers and engineers span different product teams, departments, and locations. Success requires more than an assortment of Photoshop or Sketch files, style guides, a print brand book, pattern libraries, and whatever else your team may be working from. You need a single source of truth.

Why are design systems important?

Here are just some of the things design systems help us with:

1. Efficiency and speed

Design systems allow us to work faster and more efficiently. They streamline the design and development process — decreasing the amount of time it takes to design, build, and ship new websites, products, and features. They also enable teams to rapidly prototype and experiment with ideas in high fidelity — ultimately saving the business time and money.

2. Consistency and user experience

Design systems help us design and build on-brand, quality digital products. Rather than working with a variety of styles and slightly differing approaches, teams are able to follow guidelines and stay consistent. This ensures interfaces are more predictable and accessible, which fosters trust in users and helps with conversion and retention.

3. Creating stronger brands

Design systems help weave brand identity throughout a product in a consistent and maintainable way. I'm a big believer that brand plays a crucial role in design systems. This is why I recommend thinking and designing holistically — considering the brand and product as a whole, as opposed to tackling problems one-by-one and hoping the pieces will fit.

4. They free us to focus on what matters

Design systems help designers and engineers spend less time needlessly creating the same things over-and-over — slightly differently every time — and more time focussing on user research, problem-solving, and building great products. They also help keep feedback focussed on the user experience, as opposed to debating padding, colours, and type choices.

5. Organisation

Design systems keep our work organised, which makes everything easier — from accessing common design elements in a master library, to using a uniform approach for the structure and naming conventions in the code, to ease of maintenance, iteration, and syncing of the design and code.

6. Speaking the same language

Design systems help our teams communicate more clearly by establishing naming conventions and consistent terminology across the design and code. We'll look at a simple design system model and terminology in the "Design System Model" chapter.

7. Source of truth

Design systems and documentation are a source of truth for the whole team. A well designed, implemented, and maintained design system sets high standards for your product and your process. Everyone becomes accountable for upholding these standards.

When do we need design systems?

Design systems are always useful, but the 'need' for a design system varies greatly depending on the nature of the business, product, or project.

It's a reasonably common experience for design agencies, small companies, and freelancers to design and build without a design system, then move on. This is often fine, and it works for many companies. The resulting product may be online for only a couple years before it's replaced when change is needed. There's nothing inherently wrong with that process. It's cost effective, simple, and fast.

Design systems are useful when companies aim to iteratively work on a product over time — to not just build once, and replace later. This is why they're more frequently needed for products than marketing websites.

Design systems are especially useful when a team of people are working on the same product. I can't stress this point enough.

> *"Software is often built by teams – sometimes incredibly large teams – of people. The challenge to create coherent experiences multiplies exponentially as more people are added to the mix. Also, over time, no matter how consistent or small a team is, different people will contribute new solutions and styles, causing experiences to diverge."*

Quote taken from an article **(1.1)** by Karri Saarinen **(1.2)**, a principal designer on the Airbnb design team.

Startups are a little different. For startups, a design system can be a low priority, because everything tends to be wide open to radical and fast changes of direction. They rarely have the stability, security, budget, and timeframes that established companies have. This isn't to say startups shouldn't be designing systematically; they just need to be more realistic about their priorities. That said... Start as you mean to go on! If you create a design system from the start, you'll avoid legacy problems later on.

A recent trend is to bring design and development in-house. And the larger the company, the larger the product teams (for better or worse).

My time spent working with in-house design environments/people/teams/ cultures taught me a lot about the importance of design systems, and the intricacies of designers, developers, and product managers working together.

Working on products which involve lots of people requires a different approach than projects with smaller, leaner teams. It's more complicated, and

1.1. airbnb.design/building-a-visual-language/

1.2. karrisaarinen.com

there's more that can go wrong. The expression: 'too many cooks spoil the broth' becomes a little too real at times. Every member of the team has their own preferences about what typefaces, colours, buttons, formatting, spacing, frameworks, or naming conventions you should use.

It gets messy, if you allow it.

Design systems bring structure, accountability, and order to this chaos.

Leading the way

For me, making the transition from freelance design into an in-house design leadership role was a learning experience, to say the least. Overseeing other people doing the work — or working with a team of people on the same product — is *very* different to being the one person doing the work!

Design leadership and teamwork go beyond just handing-off design mockups, style guides, and specs. You need to find a way to create — and effectively and openly communicate — common, shared design guidelines, so everyone works in the same direction. The alternative is everyone does their own thing — reinventing the wheel, bloating the code, and damaging the brand and product user experience. And sometimes, falling out in the process.

When you work on a team, your design thinking is useless if only you know about it, or if it's disruptively different from the approach of your colleagues. You need to work together in the same direction. As other chapters in this book will demonstrate, a design system genuinely helps you to do this.

The real test...

The real test of a design system is whether the design and build mirror each other, and if you and your team consistently use the elements you establish rather than needlessly creating new ones.

A successful design system liberates your team from reinventing the wheel. It allows you to focus on what really matters: learning and improving digital products to meet user and business goals. Heck, you might even create something amazing that you're all proud of!

Solving problems
is a big part of the
value proposition of
a design system.

SELL— ING A DESIGN SYSTEM

02

So far, I've talked about all the advantages a design system offers, many of which you've probably read about before. But before we get into design system models — and how to go about creating a design system — I want to take a minute to get real. Designers romanticise design systems in countless articles online, and we make it sound so easy in our case studies. But the reality is:

- They're time-consuming to build and establish.
- They take up a lot of development resources.
- They distract from working on any roadmaps of features.
- They're tricky to maintain.
- Designers can see them as a threat to their creativity.
- And, they require *a lot* of stakeholder support to succeed.

Honestly, selling a design system could well be the hardest part of the process!

You need to convince a wide range of people — from the bottom to the top of the chain of command — that it's worth it. And *it is*, but I just listed a lot of legitimate reasons not to create a design system! And these are just some of the reasons why you'll be told: "No".

To avoid being told 'No', you need to learn how to teach the value of design systems — and to earn the support and trust of stakeholders — or your design system is going to go nowhere.

Find your partner(s)

To illustrate this process, I'll share an example from my real-life experience of selling design systems at a company.

At this company, I had a partner in crime called Nick Stamas **(2.1)**. Nick had already started selling the idea of a design system before I came onboard. He had a smart approach: rather than lead with: "let's create a design system!", he gave presentations to a number of engineers from different product teams about the advantages of a centralised code base, and promoted better collaboration between designers and developers.

I was only an observer at these meetings. As a fellow design lead at the same company, I had a vested interest in this presentation going well, and I was gauging the response from the attendees. I recognised that this was the type of support and interest we'd need — to inspire, and to build — from a range of stakeholders.

In essence, Nick was sowing the seed of the idea of a design system by simply highlighting common problems most developers can identify with and tailoring his presentation to different teams. He was getting developers excited about things they care about!

To quote from an article **(2.2)** Nick wrote about this process:

> *"Sell a vision that everyone can buy in to. Selling is a process, probably more than a single meeting. Look for teaching moments. Use your storytelling skills. Show your team that a better way is possible. Come up with a memorable name and say it a lot. Get people excited with a splashy presentation."*

Aside from these presentations, Nick had made a start on a design system which he called Plasma **(2.3)**.

Nick's early approach was to begin with code — not to mock up anything in design software. He was building the bones of a code base in React by documenting basic system components like buttons and form inputs. He didn't focus on design or style. Instead, he focussed on **getting the basics right, building strong foundations, and creating a semantic system for naming conventions.**

Over time, he shared his progress with developers, one-by-one, getting them excited about it. He started inviting other developers to contribute. His intent was to prove that a simple, consistent, shared code base could be integrated and maintained effectively and efficiently within his team and product, and ultimately across different teams and in different products.

Note: Nick's advantage was his diverse development and design skillset. He spoke the same language as engineers, which helped him pitch to them. Everyone has their strengths. Play to yours, and your team's. You don't have to start a design system in code. The important message here is to get people who will be involved in the system excited about it! That often means proving your point, or earning people's trust.

2.1 nickstamas.com

2.2 uxdesign.cc/selling-a-design-system-at-your-company-74cb2bc97195

2.3 roomfive.net/plasma-design-system/

More than design and engineering

It's important to note: in these early stages, Nick was also working with his larger product team — including product managers and designers — to identify problem areas in their products and processes that the design system would address.

Solving problems is a big part of the value proposition of a design system. The more powerful stakeholders won't care about what the product looks like, or your code base. They will care about solving problems, or more specifically, the business success these solutions lead to.

'Finding your partners' involves gaining support from all stakeholders, not just designers and developers. We'll come back to Nick's story, and this process of forging partnerships, throughout this book.

Laying the foundations

In parallel to Nick's story so far — as Nick was highlighting the need for a design system — I was working on what I called the 'Digital Foundations', which we'll cover in the next chapter. For now, think of these as 'digital brand guidelines'.

These Digital Foundations were intended to act as a source of truth for our values and to guide the design, content, and build of all of the company's digital products. I based this work on the company's existing brand book*, which had been created with print and physical spaces in mind. After extrapolating what could successfully be applied to digital, I went on to greatly expand it to cover digital product requirements.

Big brands commonly create — or commission an external agency to create — a 'brand book', which acts as a 'manual' for everything created for that brand.

It's important for a large company to have brand guidelines to prevent everyone from doing their own thing, and to keep products from spiraling out of control. With the creation of these 'Digital Foundations,' our guidelines now existed, but we hadn't put them to work yet. Brand guidelines are of no use on their own. They need to be practically implemented and adhered to, and design systems give us the perfect opportunity to do so.

So naturally, after a period of shadowing each other's work, there came a point where Nick and I teamed up to collaborate on a design system. Nick directed the engineering and planning, and I led the design and creative direction. We combined the Digital Foundations with the product needs that Nick's team had brainstormed, and the code Nick had written. Working with these strong foundations, it didn't take long for an on-brand, problem-solving, and product-focussed design system to take shape.

We'll delve more into the process of creating a design system later, but for now, you can read a design case study article (**2.4**) about the Plasma design system described here.

Start small, and adjust your pitch accordingly

Continuing our story: in parallel to the design and build work, we continued to present to different stakeholders. Selling a design system never *really* stops, no matter where you are in the process. We started small, working our way up the chain of command, gaining support and momentum as we went.

It's impossible to say whether pitching the design system from top-to-bottom or bottom-to-top will work best at your company. It depends on the intricacies of different work culture, politics, personalities, and hierarchies. Have a think about which will be more effective at your company. And remember, the point is to tailor your pitch to your audience. You want to excite as many people as possible with all the ways a design system will benefit them.

From junior designers to design leads, from front-end developers to engineering leads, and from product managers to heads of departments: we spoke to a wide range of stakeholders, adjusting our pitch depending on who we were talking to. Presentations were either broad, or focussed on design and code, but they all emphasised the value of design systems. For example:

Product managers, leaders, and heads of departments...

...care about how fast the team can ship products, and the impact the work has on business goals, sales, reports, and analytics.

Sell them on how a well-established design system allows for a faster, more efficient shipping cycle. Convince them of how taking the time to create a design system now will enable faster product releases and iteration, as well as a better user experience going forward. In a 'perfect world', this increases the potential for growth, sales, and analytics trending in the right direction.

2.4 medium.com/@andrewcouldwell/plasma-design-system-4d63fb6c1afc

And remember, a really successful system will also unify the teams working with it, creating a healthier work culture, staff retention, and tool for recruiting talent. The leaders in your company *should* care about these things!

Engineers...

...care about a unified code base, version control, consistency, performance, organisation, efficiency, and naming conventions.

Sell them on how design systems will help bridge the gap between designers and developers, and their positive impact on all the engineering factors they care about. If you're not comfortable speaking their language; work with a developer on these engineering pitches.

Designers...

...care about aesthetics, brand, typography, colour, user experience, and shipping beautiful products, which stay true to their original vision.

Get them excited about how great the end product will look! Anything relating to the front-end being a 'pixel perfect' reproduction of their designs will be music to their ears. Be careful not to scare the more visual designers on your team, as some will view design systems as a threat to their creativity. Instead, focus on how quickly and efficiently they can design with pre-defined system components in their design tools of choice. The system will curb the introduction of rogue elements like buttons and form inputs, freeing them to focus on more interesting tasks like problem solving, layout, and user experience. The best designers on your team will be excited about this, and it will be a valuable learning experience for everyone else.

We're all in this together

For all parties, be sure to pitch the importance of this being a collaborative team effort. Some may worry their voice won't be heard, or that the system will go against how they like to work. A good design system won't be designed and built by *only* a few people, then closed to changes from everyone. It will evolve. It requires everyone's input and support, over time, in different capacities. It will help everyone, and it will help the business. It's something everyone should be proud of.

The following screenshot (FIG 2.1) is from a deck I used to present to an executive when I was the System Design Lead at a previous employer. This executive was not a designer or a developer, but a powerful individual with significant influence and connections. A fellow design lead at the company told me this person would be interested in the digital brand guidelines I was working on, and could be a powerful ally for our design system initiatives. With their advice, I contacted the executive, set a date/time/place for a meeting, and started preparing this presentation.

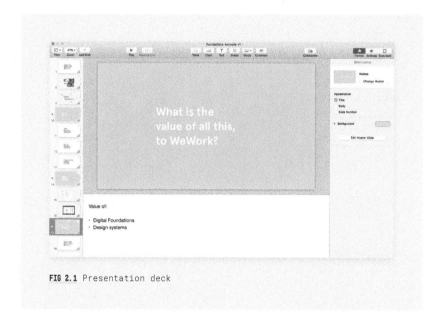

FIG 2.1 Presentation deck

This particular stakeholder didn't know or care about what designers were doing in Sketch, or how developers were refactoring code. The way to reach this person was to pitch:

- **What is the value of a design system to our company?**
- The design system saves us time and money because _____ (e.g. we can ship updates faster, as engineers won't have to write as much new code).
- The design system makes us/you look good because _____ (e.g. we can ship more updates per quarter, which could have a positive impact on sales).
- The design system sets us apart from our competition because _____ (e.g. our competition doesn't have a consistent brand across their digital platforms, so we can stand out from the crowd with a stronger brand and user experience).
- Our competitors are doing _____, which helps them because _____. (e.g. They are publicly sharing their design system, which helps them recruit a higher-caliber of designer and engineer).

- How can **you** help **us** achieve this? (e.g. We need your endorsement. And who else do you recommend we talk to, to make this happen?).

Prove to them how what you're pitching helps the company, and makes **us** (i.e. the stakeholder and the company at large) look good in the process! It's hard for managers and executives to turn down something that makes them look good, when often all they have to do is say "Yes" and grant you an endorsement and a few connections. It's a win-win for everyone.

At what stage do you sell?

This chapter on selling a design system was one of the hardest to place in this book. There is no strict linear structure to this book, but 'selling a design system' doesn't belong at the end — because you don't want to put in a lot of work only to be told "No" by someone higher up the chain of command. And it doesn't belong at the start, because you don't know yet what you're selling. You first need to understand what a design system is, why it's valuable, and what problems you're solving in order to build and present your case.

The key thing to understand is: **selling a design system isn't a stage of the process. It's ongoing.** You need to always be advocating for the system, or it will fail. Even — and perhaps especially — after you've successfully designed, built, and integrated the system.

All it takes is a powerful stakeholder to come on board and decide they don't like a systematic approach to design, and the whole thing comes crashing down. Believe me, I've seen this happen. However, if you've been gathering support throughout the conception and creation phases, the design system will have a better chance of weathering organisational changes and individuals who oppose it.

The importance and quality of 'the sell'

You need a convincing pitch to sell your vision, and you need to present it passionately and concisely — as some stakeholders' time and attention can be limited.

At large companies with more complex hierarchies *(and the politics that come with that)*, I like to think of it as being well armed before going into battle. You stand a much better chance of being taken seriously if you build up an arsenal of data, problem statements, and industry examples to demonstrate your points, as well as having the backing of a small army of supporters all champing at the bit to get started.

If you believe in design systems and want to see one thrive at your company, you need a compelling case that's tailored to your business, team, and user needs.

It's easy for higher-ups to say no. Very easy. As I mentioned earlier, creating design systems can be involved, and therefore expensive to the company.

Sometimes, projects like design systems are rejected with good reason. The more experience you get in the tech industry, the more you understand the importance of saying no. Creating new things just for the sake of having something new often leads businesses down the wrong path. Just as we shouldn't create new product features because one person 'thinks it would be cool', we also shouldn't create a design system 'because everyone else is doing it'.

So, if you believe in design systems and want to see one thrive at your company, you need a compelling case that's tailored to your business, team, and user needs. This helps your stakeholders to make informed decisions.

In the "Getting Started" chapter we'll cover how to build a compelling case by investigating what problems exist in your product and team processes, and communicating how a design system can help to solve those problems. Matching problems to a potential roadmap of solutions can be a compelling way to gain stakeholder support and turn "No" into "Yes".

A word on office politics

Every stakeholder wants something different. Some focus purely on the business needs. Some care most about customer happiness.

And — let's be honest — others may be driven by a selfish motivation. I've seen employees driven by something as trivial as taking credit, winning an award, or gaining a portfolio piece. Others have more toxic incentives, and will make poor decisions to 'earn' a promotion at the expense of their team. Unfortunately, you have to navigate these people and work around them, or find a way to make their goals fit with your broader goal of creating better products.

Here's my advice on office politics: try to understand what's *really* driving everyone involved in your product.

Your primary goal should be to rally those with pure motivations to join your cause.

- For stakeholders who care about business needs; play up the speed of iteration that comes with design systems.

- For designers who want to make something beautiful for your users; advocate for the quality output that comes with a well-crafted library of elements.
- For developers who want well-performing code; celebrate the efficiency of a consistently designed interface.

If you are passionate and well-informed, you'll build a team of like-minded advocates that can defeat any of the self-involved office politicians who might try to stand in your way.

It may also be possible to convince those who have selfish motivations that a design system will make them look good, help them win an award, or gain them the promotion they're after — in which case they could become its biggest champion. The point is to understand what's driving your stakeholders, and work with them accordingly.

Creating a design system is a process. It's a long-haul — and often expensive — project that takes up a lot of time and resources which involves more people in your organisation than just designers and developers.

It stands to reason that design systems are easier to implement at smaller organisations. A smaller design team will create less rogue design elements, and a smaller engineering team means less friction in the code base. There are also fewer people with the word 'manager' in their title, which often means there are fewer opportunities for things to go wrong. There's less need for buy-in or permission, which means there's greater potential for faster progress.

Larger organisations are a different animal. More hierarchy means more channels for decisions to go through to be approved and implemented. Think about what happens when there are dozens — even hundreds — of designers, engineers, and managers split across multiple teams, all working on the same family of products. Some of those teams may even be remote, nationwide, or international.

It gets complicated.

This isn't intended to scare you, but rather to provide a dose of reality from the trenches of my real-world experience. As I said in the beginning of this chapter, we romanticise about design systems, and we make it sound so easy. Hopefully, now that we've explored some of the challenges of creating a design system, you'll be better armed to deal with them as they arise.

I admit selling a design system is hard work, and it's not *the sexy part* that gets shared on Dribbble or Medium, but it's important.

In summary

- Start small.
- Be prepared.
- Identify the problems you're trying to solve.
- Do *some* (enough) impressive design and build work to get people talking.
- Make friends and build a team of people excited to work with you.
- Come up with a cool name, and create a *sexy* presentation.
- Tailor your pitch according to your audience.
- Earn trust and support.
- Be an advocate and a guardian for the system, and inspire others to do the same.

LAYING THE FOUND— ATIONS

03

It's easy to explain how brands and products go astray, especially nowadays with the trend of staffing huge in-house design teams with dozens of designers and engineers.

It takes a dedicated (and rare) kind of leadership to unify a team of individuals. In sport, it's the job of a coach to condition their players to adopt team tactics and play as a unit. In design and development, our teams are often so large, disparate, and constantly changing that we usually can't rely on one manager to get us all on the same page.

Instead, we can use guidelines for our brand, design, and code — as well as a clearly defined set of values and principles — to help us all work in sync.

My dad was a quantity surveyor; it was his job to evaluate building plans to assess the risk and cost required to create a solid structure. In many ways this isn't so different to what I do as a web designer and developer. Perhaps it's because of his influence that I tend to think of my work in terms of construction, and why I believe the phrase 'laying the foundations' is a great metaphor for how we should think about setting up brands, products, and teams for success.

In order for teams to work together to create great products, they need a strong foundation to build on. Just as a building built on sand won't hold up as well as one built on stable foundations, a product built with a poorly defined structure will quickly start to have issues. A solid set of guidelines and principles helps us achieve the cohesiveness, sturdiness, confidence, and scalability we need.

In this chapter, we'll focus on how to create these digital brand guidelines and principles.

Putting up scaffolding

I want to be as real as possible in this book, which is why I'm going to be blunt for a minute. As design systems become more trendy, many design articles and case studies give idealistic accounts of creating beautiful design systems, and sometimes they pass over the ugly, gritty details. This can leave many designers feeling like a systematic approach won't work for their team, because their team or product has too many issues to address. Perhaps you can't just start from scratch with a shiny new system, as many seem to do in their polished case studies.

In keeping with my construction analogy: in a perfect world, you want to 'lay the foundations', then build a beautiful 'building' (i.e. a design system and product) upon those foundations. Other times, it's just not that simple. You may have to deal with a crumbling structure that's already in place. *Out with the old and in with the new* isn't always an option.

If you've inherited a mess and your team's decided enough is enough, sometimes you can take a wrecking ball to it and clear the way for a fresh start. But what should you do if you don't have that luxury, and have to work with what you've got? In these cases, you've got to build scaffolding around your existing structure — stabilising, stopping the rot, and renovating it over time.

Worry not. Whether you're facing a nice empty plot of land, a wrecking ball, or putting up scaffolding, the principles in this chapter will help you and your team.

The importance of brand in system design

I'm a big believer that brand is a core component to a design system. It's why we spend so much time and money on building unique design systems. Without a unique brand, an off-the-shelf, white-label system (e.g. Bootstrap **3.1**) would do the job.

You likely don't want to use an open-source design system because it doesn't communicate your brand story effectively. It might have everything you 'need', but you want to create something that gives your brand a unique, strong, and focussed voice to set you apart from your competitors.

Let's look at a scenario where brand guidelines and design systems work well together.

Marketing vs. product

Product design and web design are two distinct disciplines. You can't — or arguably shouldn't — apply the same design methodologies or design systems to designing a product as you would to marketing design. Websites and products often have very different business objectives, use cases, and target audiences.

3.1 getbootstrap.com

Brand foundations help to keep everyone on the same page, speaking the same language, and working as a team — rather than a collection of individuals doing their own thing.

FIG 3.1 Dropbox brand

FIG 3.2 Dropbox marketing

FIG 3.3 Dropbox product

Take Dropbox, for example, the bright colours, extreme spacing, large buttons, and dramatic typeface Dropbox use in their brand **(FIG 3.1)** and marketing website **(FIG 3.2)** wouldn't work in their product.

Dropbox's marketing website is loud and confident, but their product succeeds by running quietly in the background — simply and efficiently. The last thing their product should be is loud, so it uses lighter colours, more compact spacing, smaller buttons, and a more reserved typeface, as seen in **FIG 3.3**.

However, some things are inherent throughout all of Dropbox's digital properties — like their use of their brand blue colour, their logo (or a compact version of it), the odd illustration, sentence case, and certain other guiding principles. Their website and product are very different, visually and functionally, but there's just enough similar about them to unify them under one brand. And that's very much by design.

Brand guidelines help companies like Dropbox unify their marketing, product, advertising, social media, copywriting, illustrations, icons, photography, and so on.

The threads that tie these different assets together need to be documented. They are the brand foundations — the pillars that run through each floor of your building, holding the whole thing together. Brand foundations help to keep all designers and engineers at a company on the same page, speaking the same language, and working as a team — rather than a collection of individuals doing their own thing.

Digital Foundations

I call these digital brand guidelines "Digital Foundations". Digital Foundations are different from traditional brand guidelines, for reasons I'll go into shortly.

Why give them the name Digital Foundations? Because it's memorable. It differentiates digital assets from other brand assets like print materials or your company's physical space. It helps to reinforce the idea of 'laying the foundations' for creating great products, and it works with our design system model*. Digital Foundations govern much of the foundational layer of the model, and guide the design of components and patterns too.

We'll delve into the design system model in the next chapter.

Traditional brand guidelines typically cover the do's and don'ts of logo, colours, art direction, brand values, and tone of voice. They are applicable to everything a company does. Some companies might publish these guidelines in a 'brand book'. Some companies produce a simple PDF.

Digital is different. The same principles we apply to physical spaces and print mediums don't always work for digital, and there are some considerations that only affect digital. Factors like accessibility and user experience impact things like the colours we use (e.g. blue for navigation, red for errors, and green for success, etc.). There are other considerations such as typography, animation, grids, responsive design, different platforms and operating systems, localisation, formatting, animation, load times, etc. which are unique to the digital experience.

Where a brand book typically comes in print or PDF forms, the ever changing nature of digital experiences requires a more — well — digital approach. Digital Foundations are better suited to a dynamic, accessible, and easily editable digital form. Some companies choose to make their digital brand guidelines public, and we'll look at a few of those in a bit. Others are private — for employee eyes only.

Let's take a look at some of the things Digital Foundations cover.

FIG 3.4 mozilla.design/overview

Mission, values, and principles

Everyone who works at your company should be aligned on what your company does, its core values, and its mission. Who is your target audience? What are your design and engineering principles? You want to align your team with a common vision, set of standards, and way of thinking.

Mozilla has a page introducing their brand, mission statement, what they stand for, and their design principles (FIG 3.4).

> *"Mozilla is the champion for a healthy internet, one that is open and accessible for all, both technologically and culturally."*

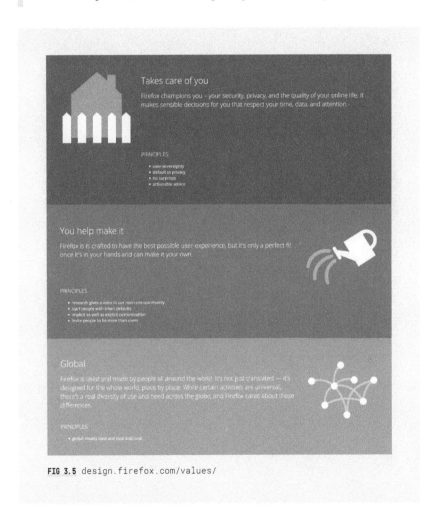

FIG 3.5 design.firefox.com/values/

Firefox, a product of Mozilla, builds upon its parent company's brand with their own design values tailored to their products **(FIG 3.5)**.

> *"As we design new features for our existing products, and create new products, we find ourselves asking — is this Firefoxy? Is what we're making a clear expression of what it means to be Firefox?"*

While it's not sourced from digital brand guidelines (or design system documentation), I'd be a fool not to share the following stellar example of mission and values in a digital space. Basic, a design agency in the United States, created a website called *Basic Culture* **(FIG 3.6)**, dedicated to sharing their 'Culture Manual'. While the content is intended for internal purposes, it's very much a statement to the outside world of 'we do awesome work, come work with us!'. Aside from the beautiful and memorable design and quirky animations, they confidently state their mission, values, and philosophies in a memorable and inspirational way — what better way is there to present such content?

FIG 3.6 culture.basicagency.com

> *"Do work you'll be proud of. Work hard while doing it. Have fun, always. Don't wait for permission. Be bold and try things. Mistakes*

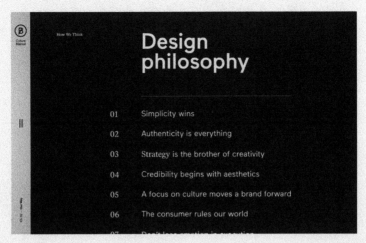

FIG 3.7 "How we think"

FIG 3.8 culture.basicagency.com/our-way/

Creating values and standards as a team is a great way to open up a positive dialogue and momentum that you can take into future design system initiatives.

happen. Learn from your mistakes. Be real. Be better. Love what you do."

I couldn't agree more with this mission statement (above).

The content you define in this section of your Digital Foundations has to come from somewhere. Perhaps your company already has something similar for the brand and company at large. If so, you should also document these values and make them accessible to your team — it all helps to foster a better understanding of the company you work for. But consider that any existing brand values may be written with consumers, business objectives, and the physical world in mind. You might want to write new values specific to design, product, technology, and a digital audience.

Early in the formation of your Digital Foundations, gather a group of people who best represent the diversity of teams working on digital products at your company — stakeholders, designers, copywriters, developers, marketing, product, etc. — and hash out your mission, values, standards, and principles. This can be an illuminating and exciting part of creating the Digital Foundations, as it reminds everyone across departments what your common goals are. Creating these shared values and standards as a team is a great way to bring people together and open up a positive dialogue and momentum that you can take into future design system initiatives.

Brand identity

Your brand identity covers everything from your logo, to typography, colour, tone of voice, photography, illustration, creative direction, motion, and so on. It answers questions such as:

- What is our logo, and how do we use it?
- What fonts and colours do we use — why, when, and how do we use them?
- Do we have any cross-platform considerations (web, iOS, Android)?
- Art and creative direction: what style of imagery do we use?
- How do we use photography, illustration, icons, animation, and video?
- Do we have any guiding principles for motion?

Uber Design **(FIG 3.9)** has a comprehensive case study page dedicated to their brand identity covering all of these topics, which forms the basis of their digital, print, and physical design systems.

Brand identity is about more than just making things look good. The colours, words, typefaces, shapes, graphics, and motion you use — and the way you use them — can make your brand more or less accessible, memorable, or relatable. Brand identities heighten the user experience, and create a familiar and consistent identity.

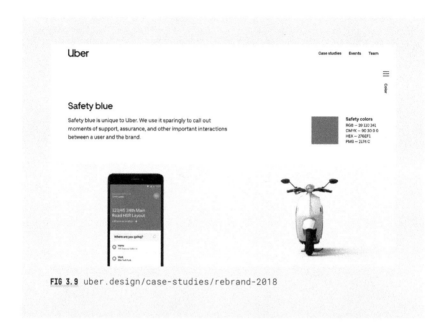

FIG 3.9 uber.design/case-studies/rebrand-2018

My personal project, Club of the Waves (FIG 3.10), is a website with a simple purpose: to showcase artists and photographers whose work focusses on surfing and surf culture. The simplicity of the concept is reflected in both it's brand identity and design system. The brand uses just three colours:

- **Black** for utility.
- Red to represent anything related to artists.
- Blue to represent anything related to photographers.

In the design system, these brand colours translate to section colour, links, buttons, the logo, hover states, filters, accent colours, and so on.

I should say — while the brand colours dictate meaning as an aid to the user experience and an embellishment — they are not required for understanding or navigation. Users can easily navigate without awareness of these colours (if they were, say, colour blind, or just don't pick up on the meaning). Accessibility considerations like this are an important distinction between Digital

Foundations and traditional brand guidelines — as we'll look at more in depth later in this chapter.

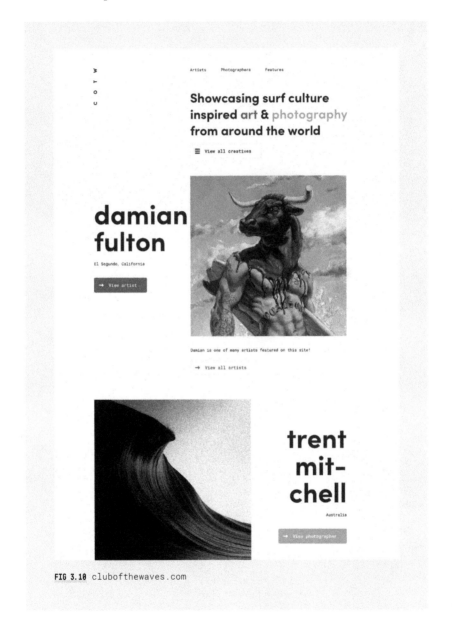

FIG 3.10 clubofthewaves.com

Google is a great example of a company with a strong and consistent brand identity **(FIG 3.11)** threaded throughout its digital properties; their simplicity, white space, clean design, logo, iconography, motion, colour, and typography make their brand instantly recognisable. Google wrote a great account **(3.2)** of how they designed their brand, and how it's intended to be used systematically across their various products.

> *"A new brand identity that makes Google more accessible and useful to our users — wherever they may encounter it."*

FIG 3.11 Google's strong brand identity

> *"The final logotype was tested exhaustively at various sizes and weights for maximum legibility in all the new digital contexts. To guide usage in screen and print, we developed standards to cover all aspects of the logotype including spacing, clearance rules, product lockups, and redline specifications for in-product treatments."*

We'll cover documenting brand identity later in this book. In the meantime, just know that having strong guidelines for your brand identity is a vital piece of your Digital Foundations.

Brand tone of voice and copywriting

How does your company want to come across to its audience? We all have our own distinct personalities and ways of talking. A brand is no different. If your designers aren't aligned on what your brand's voice and personality is, then they'll all do their own thing, and your brand voice will be weakened or lost. This is why it's vital to include copywriting guidelines in your Digital Foundations.

This interesting interview **(3.3)** with Molly Young **(3.4)** describes Warby Parker's "robust creative vision" when she joined them, and how that vision defined the tone for their copywriting:

> *"It [the Warby Parker brand] was very literary, and quirky, and fun.*
> *They had mood boards with a very specific bike, and a very specific*
> *edition of a book, and a calendar that they really liked the graphic*
> *design of. There was very specific reference points. They would*
> *describe it to me as: 'Warby Parker is the person you want to sit next*
> *to at a dinner party. They are funny and smart, and they get up to do*
> *the dishes.'"*

As their 'Director of Copy', Molly worked with Warby Parker's design team to translate this creative vision into brand copywriting guidelines.

I like this approach. Copywriting starts with brand identity and vision and is interpreted into a practical guide for its application in a digital product. These guidelines help to create more user friendly and on-brand experiences.

Molly also brings up an important point on copywriting in digital products, advising that **designers and copywriters should sit and work together:**

> *"If you put them [designers and copywriters] next to each other,*
> *they'll be looking at each other's screens and asking each other*
> *questions, and interrupting each other, and learning from each*
> *other. Once a copywriter knows how a designer thinks and vice*
> *versa, you can work together really seamlessly."*

I think this is great advice; much the same as I believe designers and developers should sit and work together. **Don't segregate your teams. Have them work together and benefit from each other's expertise.**

Another excellent article **(3.5)**, *Words Shape Design* by Joscelin Cooper **(3.6)** at Airbnb, also describes the importance of copywriters and designers working

---

3.2 design.google/library/evolving-google-identity/

3.3 link.medium.com/MlRsSmQABX

3.4 molly-young.com

3.5 airbnb.design/words-shape-design-2/

3.6 linkedin.com/in/joscelin-cooper-0262191/

together. Joscelin dispels the common (and unfortunate) expectation that a copywriters role is to:

> "...provide a word layer to already-complete designs."

Joscelin advises designers and project leads to **involve writers early**. Ideally, projects should start with a "content kickoff":

> "Getting a writer involved at the beginning means you'll start design explorations with a more informed perspective of the messages you're working to convey."

Just as new design projects benefit from early considerations for voice and tone, so should the creation of your Digital Foundations that will in-turn guide all future digital content and design projects.

Atlassian **(FIG 3.12)** introduce their brand "personality" as:

> "Our personality establishes the foundation of the Atlassian brand. It is a product of our mission, and a reflection of our culture, values, and promise to customers. We make sure that these traits come through in all of our customer-facing communications and content."

As well as defining your brand tone of voice and personality, it's good practice to define a shared vocabulary.

The Digital Foundations I created for WeWork include guidelines for brand terminology, so the team consistently uses the same language across all properties **(FIG 3.13)**. For example, all companies have 'customers' of some variety, but not all brands like to refer to them as "customers" or "clients"; instead they may use friendlier, more 'human' terms like: "members" or "guests". A popular example is using "team" instead of "staff" or "employee". Disney refer to their theme park employees as "cast members". I'm sure your company has its own preferences... If so, document them so your whole team knows about and uses them. This piece of your Digital Foundations will be especially helpful for onboarding new team members, as learning the lingo of a new company can sometimes be daunting.

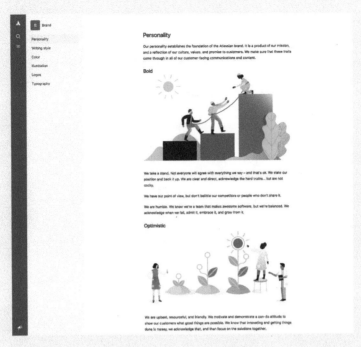

FIG 3.12 atlassian.design/guidelines/brand/personality

FIG 3.13 digital-foundations.netlify.com/brand-voice/

Formatting

In addition to tone and vocabulary, your Digital Foundations should include guidelines for formatting. For reasons we're about to examine, being consistent with punctuation, abbreviation, and language choice is vital for user comprehension and team collaboration.

Without a source of truth, your team may be unsure about something as basic as how to format a headline. Speaking from experience, you wouldn't believe how much friction a question like: "do we use sentence case or title case?" can cause across teams! *Shakes head, remembering.*

Capitalization

We use both title case ╱ and sentence case ╱ in our digital products. The guidelines below explain when to use which one:

Use Sentence Case for:

- All body copy, sentences and paragraphs.
- All captions on images, including in image galleries.
- All list items (e.g. `<ul> <li>`).
- All `Label` and `Legend` in forms, including labels on a `checkbox` and `radio` .
- All placeholder text and values on form inputs (e.g. `text-input` , `select` *etc.*).

Use Title Case for:

- All titles, headers and sub-headers (`H1` , `H2` , `H3` , `H4`).
- All buttons and calls to action.
- All text links in navigation patterns (e.g. in a global navigation bar, footer, side column navigation).
- Names, including people, companies, product names (e.g. Private Office) and places.

FIG 3.14 When do we use sentence case vs. title case?

The next few example images **(FIG 3.14 - 3.18)** are excerpts from Digital Foundations I've written in the past, including guidelines for writing everything from copy, titles, form labels, and calls to action. The screenshot above **(FIG 3.14)** is just one small piece of this documentation; it focusses on explaining when to use sentence case versus title case in various product scenarios.

Formatting guidelines could also answer questions such as:

- Do we use "and" or "&"?
- Do we put a period (".") at the end of a header?
- Do we use American English or British English?
- Do we use the Oxford comma?

To you, these questions may seem inconsequential, but when you're part of a diverse team with varied (personal) approaches to writing, the answers may not be obvious to everyone **(FIG 3.15)**.

FIG 3.15 The little details can make a big difference

For example, I live in the United States, but I'm from England. Although a good deal of my audience are undoubtedly in the United States, I made a decision to write this book in my native British English because this book is available worldwide, where British English is more commonly used. If this book was exclusively a digital product, I might decide to use American English for my audience in the United States, and British English internationally.

These things may seem trivial to some people, but if you're a San Francisco based company with a good deal of your audience outside of the United States, you should think about your approach to language and have guidelines in place.

Formatting date and time

An important factor to consider with international audiences is that the United States, Europe, and Asia all format things like date, time, and currency very differently. Don't make the mistake of assuming your international users will perceive everything the same way you do.

For example, when formatting dates (FIG 3.16):

- The United States puts the month before the day (MM/DD/YYYY).
- Europe puts the day before the month (DD/MM/YYYY).
- Asia puts the year before the month and the day (YYYY/MM/DD).

Numerical International Examples

Be aware that the format/order in which dates (day, month and year) are written, displayed or presented in form fields are very different internationally. This can easily lead to confusion in different countries if the date is presented in a way that they don't understand.

See how the 10th September 2016 is represented internationally below. You can see how it would be very easy to mix up whether the date is the 10th September, or the 9th October...

Region	Example	Format
United States	09/10/2016	MM/DD/YYYY
United Kingdom	10/09/2016	DD/MM/YYYY
Europe	10/09/2016	DD/MM/YYYY
China	2016-09-10	YYYY-MM-DD

FIG 3.16 Document formatting guidelines for dates

Take my birth date for example *(presents welcome)*: where I'm from (England), I would write my birth date as:

"24th June, 1982" or "24/06/1982"

But in the United States, I would write:

"June 24, 1982" or "06/24/1982"

Also, notice I wrote "th" after "24" in the first example... It's common practice in the United Kingdom to add an ordinal indicator (e.g. **2nd**, **3rd**, **4th**) after an ordinal number (i.e. a date), where it's less common to see ordinal indicators for dates in the United States.

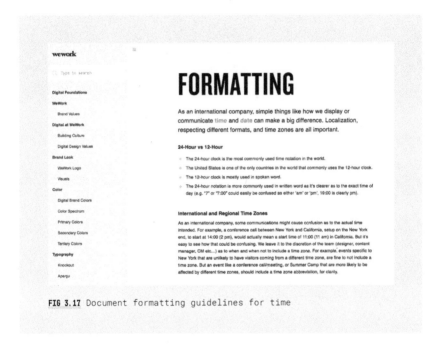

FIG 3.17 Document formatting guidelines for time

As for time: the United States (U.S.) is one of the only countries in the world not to use the 24-hour clock (they use the 12-hour clock). Those not living in the United States would understand that 09:00 is 9 in the morning, where 21:00 is 9 in the evening — but a good deal of people in the U.S. would need to see 9:00 a.m. or 9:00 p.m. to make sense of these times. This is important, both for companies in the U.S. building products that are used abroad, and for companies outside of the United States targeting a U.S. audience.

Similarly, the east and west coasts of the United States are in different time zones. If your target audience is nationwide in the U.S., being specific about time is important. If you state that a game kicks off at 7:30 p.m., but don't specify 7:30 p.m. EST (Eastern Standard Time), your audience on the west coast (in the Pacific Standard Time zone) are gonna be pretty mad when they tune in 3 hours too late!

Time and date are tricky. There are *so many* different ways you can represent both. When we look at something called 'interface audits' later in this book, you may be surprised by how many different formats you find in your product for time and date. If you're referencing time, for example, you could write:

- "1 hour ago"
- "1 hr ago"
- 1h ago
- 1h

A quick browse through several news websites shows how many different formats are used to express the exact same time and date. The following examples are real:

- Feb 1, 2019
- February 01, 2019
- 1 February 2019
- 1st February 2019, 4:04 pm
- February 1, 2019, at 4:04 p.m.
- February 1 2019, 4:04pm
- Feb. 1, 2019 4:04 p.m. ET
- Feb. 1, 2019, 4:04 PM EST
- Fri 1 Feb 2019 16.04 GMT
- 4:04 PM ET, Fri February 1, 2019
- 16:04 EST, 1 February 2019

Given that there are *so many* different ways to format things like dates, times, numbers, and currency; including do's and don'ts and example scenarios in your Digital Foundations can provide a valuable distinction for clarity sake.

The Google Material documentation **(3.7)** also has a section on best practices for formatting date and time.

Now that you've got a better sense of the importance of documenting these seemingly small details, I hope you're motivated to include formatting guidelines in your Digital Foundations.

3.7 material.io/design/communication/data-formats.html

Don't assume your international audience perceives everything the same way you do.

Accessibility and inclusivity

Ideally, your company should already understand the importance of accessibility in their digital products. If not, I recommend reading: *Planning for Accessibility* **(3.8)** by Laura Kalbag **(3.9)**, which outlines a number of considerations to 'make the case for accessibility — to yourself, coworkers, bosses, and clients'. Laura has also written a book **(3.10)** on accessibility. And I put together a list **(3.11)** of accessibility resources and tools on this book's website that you may find useful. *So now you have no excuses! ;)*

Maybe you're not sure why accessibility and inclusivity are that big of a deal? Well, consider that accessibility isn't just about disabilities and impairments, but also people of different ages (young and old), and people who speak a different language. We're talking about a potentially very large audience!

There are several business benefits to creating more accessible products. For example:

- A more accessible e-commerce product will have fewer sales fall through, and fewer community support and help enquiries and complaints.
- You could expand your reach to a larger audience, giving you a competitive edge over your competitors.
- If nothing else, you probably care about not being sued for discrimination! Depending on the countries and/or industries you operate in, an accessible site may be required by law. Think about shops providing disabled access via ramps and lifts/elevators, as opposed to (or in addition to) steps... Your online shop is not so different.

Simple accessibility issues include:

- Use of colour. Think about colour blindness. The contrast between text and background colour can affect the legibility and visibility of text.
- How do you distinguish links, warnings, and changes of state? If you're relying only on a change of colour to indicate something, be aware that some people won't see that change of colour. Instead, try more explicit states — and changes of state — like an underline, or a different weight/ size/position.
- Form inputs should always have a label. Without a label, an input (on its own) is most likely meaningless to a screen reader.
- If you use icons on their own, without an accompanying text label — what does the icon mean? This is as much a user experience, cultural, and common sense thing, as it is an accessibility issue.
- Think about people who use screen readers, or navigate websites with a

keyboard, as opposed to a mouse or trackpad. Not everyone navigates and consumes content the same way.
- Do you rely on sound to convey something important? Not everyone can hear.

When we talk about accessibility and inclusivity, we're not just talking about designing for disabilities and impairments, we're talking about everyone.

For example, physical (and mental) attributes deteriorate as we age. Of course it depends on your business and target audience, but is excluding people above a certain age wise for your business? As Don Norman **(3.12)** puts it in his excellent article **(3.13)**:

> *"The number of active, healthy oldsters is large–and increasing. We are not a niche market. And businesses should take note: we are good customers often with more free time and discretionary income than younger people."*

Especially when designing for touchscreens and mobile devices, we should consider things like small text being harder to read, or small touchpoints and/or touch-sensitive interactions being difficult to action as eye-hand coordination declines, or when people are on the move. Have you ever watched an older family-member try to perform a 'force touch' on a screen or trackpad... *Yeah, good luck explaining that interaction!* "Press it, but don't press hard — just a little bit... No, too hard!".

> *"Are elderly people handicapped? Maybe, but so is a young, athletic parent while carrying a baby on one arm and a bag of groceries in the other (and perhaps trying to open their car door)."*

3.8 alistapart.com/article/planning-for-accessibility/

3.9 laurakalbag.com

3.10 abookapart.com/products/accessibility-for-everyone

3.11 designsystemfoundations.com/resources/

3.12 jnd.org

3.13 fastcompany.com/90338379/i-wrote-the-book-on-user-friendly-design-what-i-see-today-horrifies-me

If you haven't put any accessibility standards in place already, you should research what you can do, start a discussion with your team, review your products, and take steps to improve your product's accessibility. It's a fascinating subject, and you may be surprised at what you learn and how much of a difference you can make.

FIG 3.18 microsoft.com/design/inclusive/

Use your Digital Foundations to document your standards, raise awareness by educating your team on accessibility issues in digital design, and write guidelines for how to design for accessibility.

Microsoft has a comprehensive page **(FIG 3.18)** in their digital design guidelines on their dedication to inclusive design, including their principles, resources, toolkits, and case studies.

Small changes can make a big difference. Consider making inclusive design a part of your team's design and product thinking.

Responsive design

Hopefully, you and your design team are already working 'responsively', but if you're not sure what I mean by this, don't worry — you're not alone. I've worked on many teams where some of the designers weren't sure how to design with different browser widths and/or devices in mind. If this describes you, or someone on your team, pause here to read — or recommend — my article **(3.14)** on responsive web design, which covers best practices for incorporating responsive web design into your design process.

If you're already designing with responsive layouts in mind, you should document any responsive grids you use in your products, and best practices for designing responsively.

Responsive design is a problem area I've experienced at many companies. You may be surprised how little some web designers know about responsive design — don't take anything for granted. Instead, use your Digital Foundations as a platform to educate your team and get everyone on the same page about designing for all screen sizes and devices.

Google Material **(FIG 3.19)** does a great job of documenting the makeup of their responsive layout grid by clearly defining the makeup and terminology of a responsive grid.

Material clearly documents what 'columns', 'gutters', and 'margins' are, and how they work across different breakpoints. Their guidelines explain percentage width columns versus fixed pixel (px) values, and flexible columns versus fixed gutter widths.

3.14 medium.com/owl-studios/responsive-design-af7a1f14b991

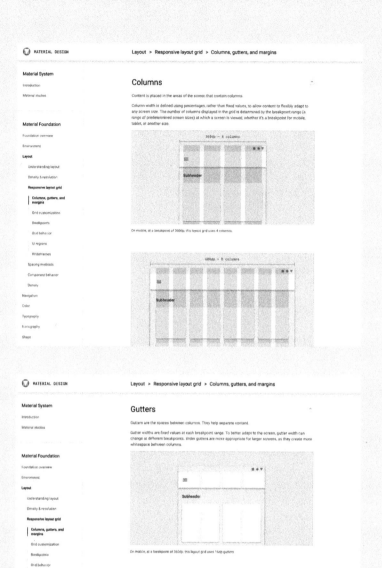

FIG 3.19 material.io/design/layout/responsive-layout-grid.html

Process

Document your design, engineering, and even interviewing processes so everyone knows what is expected. You might even document things like naming conventions for files and folder structure, to keep things organised.

How does your team approach a design problem, and answer questions like:

- From design thinking, brainstorming, sketching, wireframing, initial ideas, design mockups, design critiques, to design hand-off... What do you do?
- Who is responsible for what?
- How do designers and engineers work together?
- How do you go from design to code?

You should have a clear process for making iterations or additions to a design system, so everyone knows things like:

- How is it decided what your team works on?
- How and where do you keep track of tasks, to-dos, and so on?
- Have you updated the design library, as well as the code?
- Have you updated the documentation with the latest change?

If you're not sure of the answers to these questions, then that's proof you need to discuss these topics — and document the answers and processes you agree on (i.e. your Digital Foundations) — with your team. Anything you can do to align your team on process is a good thing. Think about the benefit to new team members who need to rapidly familiarise themselves with your team's processes, or how a source of truth will help align your team on design process and workflows.

Design systems

Your Digital Foundations are guidelines for all the best practices that fall outside of — and dovetail into — your actual design system(s), such as brand identity, tone of voice, process, etc. Relating to design systems, your Digital Foundations should be a source of truth and answer questions like:

- Does your team follow a specific model or methodology for design systems? In the next chapter, I'll introduce you to a simple design system model. If you choose to follow that model — or for whatever methodology you use — you should outline it in your Digital Foundations, so everyone is on the same page.

- Do you use specific terminology to describe different aspects of your design system?
- Why are design systems valuable to different teams at your company? You could repurpose any pitches you've used while 'selling your design system', as referenced in the previous chapter, to empower other team members to advocate for the adoption of design systems.

Your company may have more than one design system (one for marketing websites, one for mobile apps, one for employee-facing products, one for customer-facing products, etc.), so these guidelines should be general enough to set the foundation for all your design systems. To unify them under one brand, and to ensure when your teams collaborate across different products, teams, and departments, that they are speaking the same language — using the same vocabulary and methodologies. From these Digital Foundations for design systems, you can also link to any design system documentation and resources, if applicable.

How are Digital Foundations different to design system documentation?

As stated earlier with the Dropbox example, some things are inherent throughout all of a brand's digital properties (across marketing websites, products, apps, and so on). Each property can be very different — visually and functionally — but Digital Foundations help to unify a brand across all its digital experiences. A company can have Digital Foundations *and* a design system; some companies even have multiple design systems to cover different products, each with their own documentation.

Digital Foundations are more all-encompassing, covering brand identity, formatting, and "a shared vocabulary for design", as IBM puts it **(FIG 3.20)**. Design system documentation is more specific — it covers components and patterns created using the Digital Foundations as a starting point, but is specifically for use in a particular website or product.

For example, IBM's Carbon design system **(FIG 3.21)** was built upon the foundations of their "IBM Design Language" **(FIG 3.20)** brand guidelines.

Once their "IBM Design Language" guidelines (or their version of Digital Foundations) were in place, they had a strong foundation on which to build their design system.

FIG 3.20 ibm.com/design/language/

FIG 3.21 carbondesignsystem.com

Make it visible, make it count

Most importantly, your team needs easy access to these Digital Foundations. **The more accessible they are, the more likely your team are to adopt, understand, and even — ideally — contribute to them.**

The way you present or document these guidelines, values, and principles will have a big impact on their adoption. It might be smart to brainstorm with your team how to proceed. Get them involved and excited about it.

It doesn't have to (just) be a website, digital document, or a wiki — it could be something visual in the physical space.

Percolate, a marketing platform in New York City, put up posters **(FIG 3.22)** around their office as a reminder of their values.

> *"Our mission and vision keep us aligned to a common goal. Each value is paired with a question that anyone within Percolate could ask themselves, to help them understand whether the decision they're making is aligned with the company."*

Your brand, design, and engineering principles are the mantra that guide everything you do. They are the driving force and inspiration. With every foundation, component, pattern, template, web page, or banner you design, and with each header and paragraph you write, ask yourself: **"Does this align to our brand principles?"**

FIG 3.23 focuslabllc.com/standards

Focus Lab, a design agency in the United States, created a series of posters
(FIG 3.23) highlighting their design standards and hung them prominently
around their studio space.

> *"We have a collection of standards that we strive to live up to each
> day. We reference them just about every week in one way or another.
> They've become part of our lexicon in the office."*

It's an interesting idea: to present design values, principles, and standards in
the physical world — not just digitally. We are very passive in our consumption
of most things digital. It's easy to forget a website, or never revisit it.

Presenting design guidelines in the real world — in poster form (FIG 3.24), a
desktop calendar, a sketchbook, a coaster, a desktop/phone wallpaper, and so
on — might be a brilliant way of getting people to notice and remember.

My former colleague, Keaton Price **(3.15)** came up with a cool idea to reinforce our design team's values — by presenting them as an award **(FIG 3.25)**. He designed a beautiful postcard, and distributed a limited number of these cards to each team member. The idea was: if you experienced a member of the team exemplifying one of the team's core values, then you would tick the value(s) they exhibited, write them a personal message, sign it, and present it to them as an award. I can tell you from the perspective of someone who both received and gave these awards that it was a great feeling, and did wonders for team and personal morale too! It put a smile on someone's face, showed gratitude and team spirit, and reinforced our team's values. Win-win!

3.15 keaton.design

3.16 google.com/docs/about/

And it doesn't just have to be stating standards and values. You could get creative — presenting other foundations like brand colours, typography, formatting reminders, art direction, and so on.

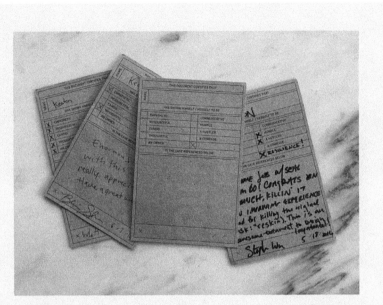

FIG 3.25 Design team values presented as awards

Just get it done!

It's easy to get caught up in the presentation of things — sometimes, so much so that we delay or even don't do the things we wanted to do! As designers, we want to create something beautiful and memorable. As developers, we're tempted to build everything ourselves. I faced this very problem on both fronts (as a designer and developer) when I first set out to create Digital Foundations. I was tempted to design and build a website as a vehicle for the content — but the content was practically bursting out of me, waiting to be written — so I decided it was daft to let design and code stand in the way of progress.

My solution seemed so simple, yet so effective. I just opened a new Google Doc **(3.16)**, and started writing. The content flowed out, free from the distraction of design software or code editors. Plus, a Google Doc is easy to share with your team; they can contribute, comment, suggest edits, and invite more team members to join. It's easy to reference from anywhere, on any device, even offline. It does almost everything you need it to do!

Here is a screenshot **(FIG 3.26)** from the Digital Foundations I created, in a Google Doc:

FIG 3.26 Digital Foundations in a Google Doc

Of course, it's hard to get excited about a Google Doc. So in the longer term, the Digital Foundations evolved into a more visually compelling and engaging entity (as a website), but the Google Doc did its job well, for a long time. It's worth considering.

Again, don't let technology or design ego stand in the way of getting your Digital Foundations produced and out there with your team. The longer they stay unwritten, the longer your product woes will persist.

We'll talk more about Google Docs in the "Document everything!" chapter, later in this book.

Flaunt it

It's not uncommon for companies to make their Digital Foundations or design system documentation public. This may seem like a strange decision...

FIG 3.27 uber.design/case-studies/rebrand-2018

Surprising and intentional

Our new illustration, motion and photography systems act as the perfect counterpoint to the standardized core brand elements. These expressive parts of our brand are more organic and playful while still communicating a message.

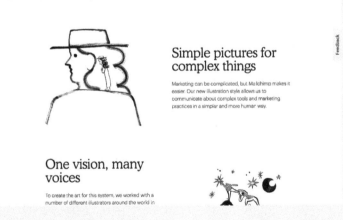

FIG 3.28 mailchimp.com/design/

It's kinda like putting an instruction manual online for everyone to see, for something only you use. However, it actually has its advantages.

Digital Foundations are the best and most idealistic representation of your brand. They are what your company aspires to be, what it wants to look like, and how it wants to make people think or feel. Presented well, they can paint a brand in a positive light. They can even paper over the cracks — and let's be honest, some tech companies need any good press they can get! Design can offer these companies a great opportunity to look good in the public domain.

Internally, the objective should be to align your team(s) on how you design and build products.

Externally, it's *showbiz*. It's a confident move. It says: 'We're proud of the great work our team does. We're awesome. Come work with us!' And it works! Digital Foundations can be a great recruiting tool, and they can be great for public relations. They can be beautifully designed, sexy, colourful, loud, or animated. They can make the company look awesome, and they're a great talking point on social media and in design case studies.

Uber Design **(3.17)** hired outside help from a respected design agency, Ueno **(3.18)** to help create and publically showcase their brand guidelines. Together they created a splashy website **(FIG 3.27)** to really maximise their impact and reach.

MailChimp Design **(FIG 3.28)** opted for a simpler, one-page website to showcase their 2018 redesign/brand. It's part business promotion, part flexing design muscle, and part recruitment tool. This approach can cost very little to do if you do it internally.

Another growing trend for highlighting design and engineering at tech companies is to showcase a limited amount of digital brand guidelines alongside articles and case studies. Some even offer free design resources, downloads, podcasts, and interviews.

Airbnb Design **(FIG 3.29)** and Microsoft Design **(FIG 3.30)** both do something like this.

3.17 uber.design

3.18 ueno.co/work/uber-design

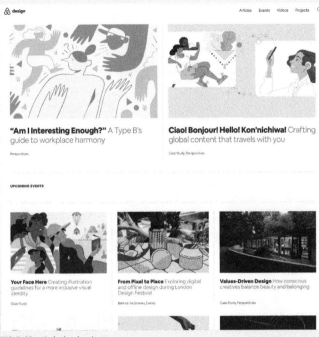

FIG 3.29 airbnb.design

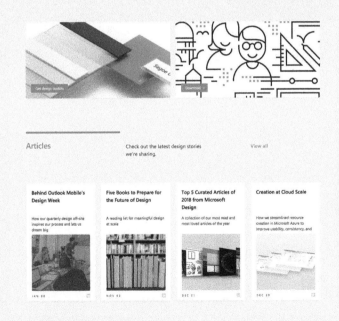

FIG 3.30 microsoft.com/design/

Don't lose sight of why you're doing this...

Publishing your Digital Foundations for the world to see is a choice. It can be great for public relations, and it can be a great recruitment tool. But the most important thing is that you lay these foundations internally at your company for the benefit of your team(s) and your product(s). Outside attention is *not* the core reason for doing them.

And keep in mind that the public brand guidelines you see online may be more for show than anything — so by all means use them for inspiration, but don't lose sight of your team's particular needs, or let your desire to create something flashy get in the way of creating something useful.

With your Digital Foundations laid, let's look at creating a design system!

The more accessible your Digital Foundations are, the more likely your team are to adopt, understand, and even (ideally) contribute to them.

DESIGN SYSTEM MODEL

04

The previous chapter talked about laying strong foundations for digital products at a company by establishing digital brand guidelines. With those foundations in place, we're ready to start building an on-brand design system that combines our brand and digital guidelines with the user and business needs.

Let's start with the basics by defining some terminology and looking at a simple model for creating design systems.

Speaking the same language

The Internet is flooded with information on design systems, and I encourage you to read as much as you can. However, the more you read about design systems, the more you realise that everyone uses different terminology to describe the same or similar things. This starts to get very confusing, especially when you're trying to get other people (aka stakeholders) on board with the idea of creating a design system.

Speaking the same language is very important when working with teams. Communication is hard enough without adding different definitions for different design system terms to the mix. So at the very least, you need to align on what terminology you're all using.

One thing to always keep in mind: **the less jargon you use, the better**.

Communication made easy

Following one design system model is a great way to keep your team on the same page as to what each part of the system represents. A simple model will also assist you in selling the concept of design systems to stakeholders.

Also, the simpler the language you use in your design system model, the easier it will be to communicate. As covered in the previous chapter, you should define the (design system) terms your team is using in your Digital Foundations, or at least in your design system documentation.

For example, you may have heard design system lingo like: foundation, component, pattern, atom, molecule, and organism. But the thing is: after you've read a few articles and spoken to a few different people, you realise that people draw their own conclusions as to what each term means based on their use in a variety of different contexts. With an industry the size of tech — spanning international borders, languages, and cultures — it's easy for the meaning of terms to diverge.

This confusion is unavoidable, industry-wide. But it is avoidable on your team(s). It's an inefficient use of time and a frustrating experience for all to have to continually explain terminology to people and then debate which term is better, so **it's important your team(s) align on a model, and a shared language**. The same goes for any naming conventions used in the design and code of a design system.

Not everyone knows what you know

It's easy to recommend you create Digital Foundations *(see previous chapter)* and to define the terminology of this model as a source of truth that's accessible by everyone on the team. But not everyone sees your documentation. Not everyone reads the same articles you do, attends the same conferences, or shares your experience. And as much as I'd like them to, not everyone will read this book *(though by all means, buy them all a copy!)*.

I've made the mistake a few times of dropping design system lingo into conversations where there wasn't a shared understanding of terminology, and it's caused confusion and frustration. The lesson I learned is not to assume everyone knows what you know. It's a simple and somewhat obvious lesson, but we're all guilty of it in one way or another.

Here's a simple way I got my team using the same terminology: in presentations to department heads, product managers, and designers *(referring back to the "Selling a Design System" chapter)*, I would often start by briefly introducing what design systems are, and the model and terminology I was proposing we use. It's no use launching into a pitch if the people you're addressing don't understand what you're talking about.

I made this mistake again, later, when I assumed the engineering team(s) would know all about design systems, and that they'd be totally on board with the concept. I was wrong, at least about the knowing part.

I remember having a productive and enthusiastic chat about our plans for creating a design system with an Engineering Lead. He *got it*. Everything. We we were on the same page. But I was somewhat surprised when the meeting ended with him asking me to schedule a presentation to our engineering teams, which, at the time, was dozens of people scattered around the planet! He asked me to explain to them what design systems are, to introduce them to the model and terminology, and to help them understand why we should invest time in any of it.

It's important
your team aligns
on a design system
model and a
shared language
that everybody
understands. The
less jargon you use,
the better.

Thankfully the presentation went well. Aligning everyone on the same page got them excited about the project, and helped me earn their support. I was also able to answer any questions, dispel any concerns, and gain a lot of momentum.

Aligning on a model and terminology

Back in 2016, I became a 'Design System Lead' at a large company and was tasked with launching a department-wide system design initiative for teams that hadn't worked with design systems before. While researching a design system model and terminology to use, I was confused by the many different terms — and jargon — I found to describe and break down a design system. Call me stubborn, but since what I found was too complicated, I created my own! My goal with creating this model was to give the team a set of easy-to-understand terms that we could all start using with as little friction as possible.

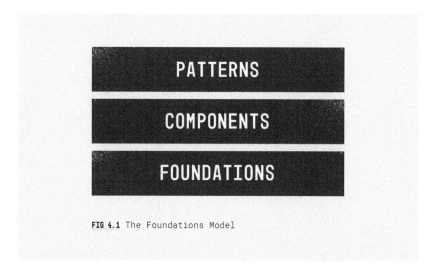

FIG 4.1 The Foundations Model

The Foundations Model

Please feel free to use this model at your company, but don't be afraid to change the terminology to suit your team's preferences. The most important thing is that you all understand and feel comfortable with it!

I call it the 'Foundations Model' **(FIG 4.1)**.

I came across the term 'foundations' a few times in my research. Its use case was a little different every time, but as I mentioned in the previous chapter, I thought it was a great analogy for how to approach system design. In construction, foundations are crucial to a building's stability, quality, and longevity — and the same applies to building digital products. To reiterate what I said earlier:

A building built on sand will only stand for so long. You need to lay strong foundations, before you build anything.

I've already shared my love of using construction analogies, but I really think it's no coincidence we use terms like 'building' in digital design. There are many parallels between the construction and tech industries — from architecture and design, to engineering and development, to quality assurance, deployment, marketing, and maintenance.

In line with keeping things simple and easy for people to understand, it's helpful to think in visual terms. You could look at the design system model (**FIG 4.1**) as a building made up of building blocks. Each level expands upon, integrates with, and is built upon the level below.

It's also important to consider: there are many other factors involved in the process of creating or iterating on a design system (**FIG 4.2**). User experience, data, accessibility, content strategy, localisation, user testing, and brand should all be interwoven in every level of your design system model. They are

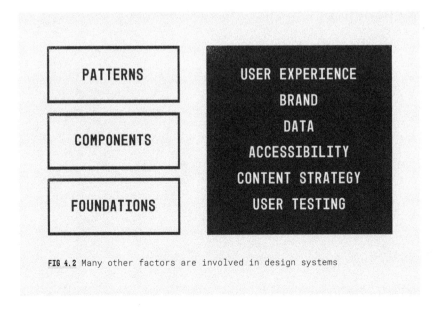

FIG 4.2 Many other factors are involved in design systems

the glue, the cement, the beams, and the pillars that hold the model together, and make it great.

Let's get into what each level of our design system model is.

Foundations

As we covered in depth in the previous chapter, your Digital Foundations should be the basis for every digital project you do, including your design system(s). Foundations are multifaceted and arguably more extensive than the other levels, which is why they warranted their own chapter. There's a reason the model is named after this foundational layer.

To review, Digital Foundations include the subjects that brand guidelines typically cover, such as guidelines for the identity, typography, text styles, colour, icons, photography, imagery, and illustration. They also cover less visual aspects like brand tone of voice, formatting choices, and things like brand values and design and engineering principles.

FIG 4.3 Foundations example: text styles

Digital Foundations also go beyond brand to span design and code issues, with guidelines for calls to action and links, layout and spacing, formatting of date, time, and currency, localisation, responsive grids, animation, and accessibility.

Foundations can be extensive or brief, depending on the size and complexity of your product suite. As I mentioned in the previous chapter, your Digital Foundations are guidelines for things (such as brand values, logo treatment, formatting, etc.) that cover all your digital properties. However, other aspects of your foundations may only be specific to one digital property — for example, your company's marketing site may use a responsive grid, but your desktop or mobile app/product may not. Or, it's not uncommon for different digital properties to use fonts unique to them (think back to the Dropbox example in the previous chapter). In these cases, you may have foundations that are unique to the design system created for each digital property. Be sure to include any property-specific guidelines — along with the company-wide Digital Foundations you've already created — in your design system documentation.

A simple example of property-specific foundations are a set of text styles for a website, which are different to those used in a mobile app. Defining a limited set of text styles for headers, copy, quotes, captions, and so on is wise for consistency and user experience, as well as a streamlined code base. The example **(FIG 4.3)** shows two responsive text styles designed specifically for headers and subheaders.

Components

These are the smaller building blocks of a digital product. Components are

FIG 4.4 Components example: a text input

distinctive user interface (UI) elements that are used repetitively throughout a product. For the most part, they are actionable or at least used to convey meaning.

Examples include: buttons, form inputs, selects, textareas, radio buttons, checkboxes, range sliders, toggles, avatars, tooltips, and so on. The following (FIG 4.4) shows a text input component and all its states.

It's good practice to not get too carried away with creating completely bespoke components — for the most part, there's rarely a need to reinvent the wheel with these. There's a good reason why selects (i.e. a form input with an arrow, which opens a dropdown menu on-click) look the same on most websites: people can instantly identify their function. This commonality, consistency, and familiarity in digital interfaces are important, not boring. Using conventional components (that aren't 'overstyled') makes sure that inputs and actionable items are instantly recognisable to users. It also makes it easier for developers to build an accessible and consistent solution that works across a variety of devices and browsers which isn't too complicated or code heavy.

Take the example below (FIG 4.5):

FIG 4.5 One of these is more identifiable than the other

The component on the left is unmistakably a select — we know that if we click the input, or the arrow, we will see a dropdown with more options. The component on the right, however, could be mistaken for a button, or it could be overlooked entirely as a non-actionable, purely decorative element. If this were an e-commerce website, can you afford for some users to miss this component and leave without making a purchase?

Patterns

These are the larger building blocks of a digital product. Patterns refer to recurring or ever-present elements or practices throughout a product. A pattern can often be comprised of established foundations and components

— for example, a card pattern may feature a header and a description, using a couple of different text styles (foundations), and a button (component).

Examples include: navigation, footer, modals, alerts, notifications, tables, feed cards, product cards, image galleries, carousels, feature or masthead areas, pagination, breadcrumbs, and so on. The example below **(FIG 4.6)** shows a responsive image gallery pattern:

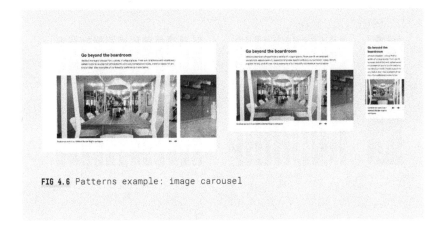

FIG 4.6 Patterns example: image carousel

Even specific layouts or content blocks can be patterns — for example, a simple, repeatable lock-up of image and text, like the example pattern below **(FIG 4.7):**

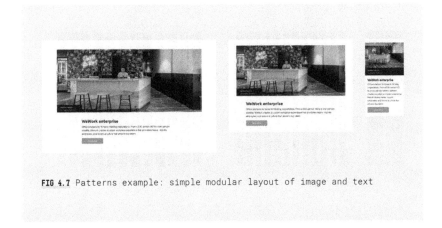

FIG 4.7 Patterns example: simple modular layout of image and text

Patterns can also refer to less tangible factors, such as your philosophy for how pages and content should load, your use of error states and animations, or what happens with empty states, onboarding, and guiding tips throughout a product.

Patterns are often modular, meaning they're designed to pair well with other patterns to tell marketing stories, sell products, present content, cross-sell, and so on.

Templates and Pages

Foundations, components, and patterns make up the basis of this design system model, but their application is just as important as the elements themselves. If foundations, components, and patterns are the building blocks, then you need schematics to pull it all together, which is where the following additional layers of the model come in.

When designing a mainly content-driven website (as opposed to digital products or apps, which I'll address shortly), I refer to these additional layers as 'templates' and 'pages' (FIG 4.8):

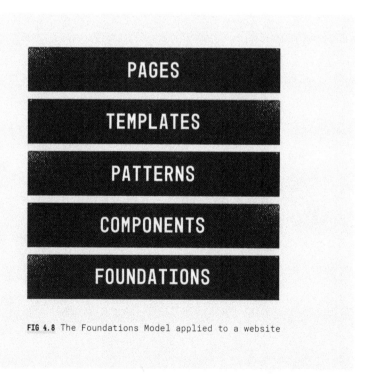

FIG 4.8 The Foundations Model applied to a website

Let's look at these two new layers in depth.

Templates

In digital terms, a template is a consistent layout that is used multiple times throughout a website, and are populated with different content each time they're used. Common examples of templates include an article or a blog post.

Consistency in web design is important for good user experience — not just for style, but also for the way content is presented. It's good practice to have as few templates as possible, so people can familiarise themselves with the interface as quickly as possible. If somebody needs to keep re-learning what's going on — where to look or click for every new template they encounter — they're highly likely to get frustrated. And frustrated customers don't stay customers very long!

Using fewer templates is also a consideration for development, maintenance, and scalability. The fewer templates you use, the easier and less expensive the build and maintenance will be. For example, adding a new employee profile page using an existing template is significantly faster and easier than building a bespoke page for each new person you hire. Making global, sweeping changes to a website is easier when you update a single template, which automatically updates multiple pages. Imagine what a nightmare it would be to make a global change to the New York Times or BBC websites, if each of their articles had a bespoke page design, as opposed to using the same, or a limited number of template(s).

Pages

Pages are essentially the final application of the design system at work. They're what your audience ultimately sees.

A page is either the application of a template, or a bespoke one-off web page. Sometimes it's good for certain pages to differentiate and not come from a template, such as when you need them to communicate a bespoke message or perform a specific function. Pages like the home page or a contact page are good examples of bespoke pages.

For an example of the relationship between templates and pages, consider the design system I created for Club of the Waves, a website featuring surf artists and photographers, each of whom has their own unique profile page on the site.

The image below **(FIG 4.9)** shows templates (only two) in the left column, and pages to the right:

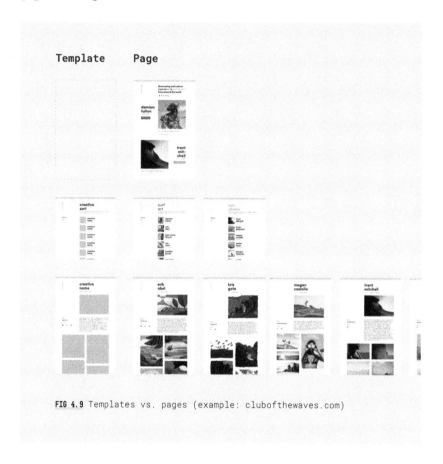

FIG 4.9 Templates vs. pages (example: clubofthewaves.com)

Club of the Waves has a bespoke home page, with no template applied to it — as seen in the first row of the image above.

The second row shows the template for an index of profiles, and two pages (to the right of it) with that template applied to them. The third row shows the template for individual profiles, and several pages (to the right of it) with that template applied to them.

In Club of the Waves' case, there are hundreds of pages running off the one profile template. It would be unrealistic to design and build a bespoke page for every creative profile, and a nightmare to make global changes to each unique page. But with all the pages running off the one template, you need only update the one template to change every page — for example, if you wanted to add a comments section or social sharing links to all profile pages.

The same logic applies to all aspects of a design system. For example, if you update a system component like a button, the change would be applied everywhere that button is used in the system. This is much easier than the lengthy and hazardous task of digging for and updating all of the buttons. *The system at work!*

Design systems in product design

As I stated before, the model's terminology is flexible. For example, where the Foundations Model terminology we've covered thus far — foundations, components, patterns, **templates**, and **pages** — works best for web design, the following terminology is arguably more appropriate for product design (FIG 4.10).

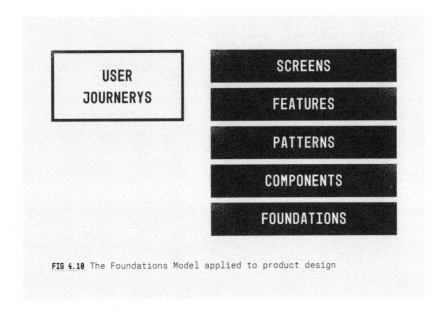

FIG 4.10 The Foundations Model applied to product design

'Templates' and 'pages' can be applicable to products too, but 'features' and 'screens' are arguably more applicable terms when designing a system for a more complex or dynamic digital product or app.

'User journeys' map out the often complex interactions within a product's features. And 'screens' are snapshots in time of a product in use (i.e. a step in the user journey). I'll demonstrate this using a real product in a moment, but first, consider this:

Websites are often about consuming content, and only include quite simple interactions like clicking a button to go to a different page, submitting a form, filtering a list to make a selection, or opening an accordion. Products and apps, on the other hand, tend to be more multi-layered, with interactions that can go several layers (or steps) deep.

For example, a banking product might have a 'screen' dynamically created and tailored to a specific user account, user type, and preference settings. This already sets it apart from a 'page', because the format and content of these dynamic screens might have dozens of possible outcomes and resulting feature sets. For example, a single screen in a banking product may include the ability to transfer money between accounts, set up a wire transfer, pay a bill, view statements, download data, open a new account, and so on.

Where typical patterns or templates in web design are not so complicated, each of our banking example's features may require more than one or two clicks to set in motion. Each feature can have a multi-step 'user journey' to perform certain tasks. In a way, you could look at features as being 'super patterns', but that name doesn't hold much credibility. On the surface, a feature is an assortment of foundations, components, and patterns — pulled together to perform a specific task(s). But each interactive part of a feature can go several layers deep, creating more of a user journey.

To give a more specific example, let's say a banking product has a feature that enables you to get directions to your local bank branch. A potential user journey for this feature might be:

1. The user clicks a button that reads: "Find your nearest bank"
2. A modal opens where the user is asked to enter their postal/zip code
3. Upon submit, a map is revealed showing banks near their location
4. The user clicks on their desired pin on the map
5. A tooltip opens with a link to directions
6. The user clicks the link and is directed off-site to Google Maps
7. And finally, for each of the previous steps you could have multiple success states, error states, helpful tips to guide the user, micro-interactions, and so on.

The bottom line is: digital products are complicated! It's vital that your system include not just all of the elements involved in the example above (e.g. buttons, modals, maps, pins, tooltips, etc.), but that it also maps out how a feature is used — showing all of the screens that add up to the user's journey. *(Doing this may also reveal some opportunities to simplify the experience!).*

To reiterate my earlier point, despite this complexity, you still need a somewhat simple model that people can get on board with. If 'features', 'screens', and 'user journeys' don't resonate with you, then re-work the model to work for your product and team. The main thing is not to overlook the various parts of the system that make up your products.

A case study of a design system at work

Let's look at the design system I created for the Adobe Portfolio product (**4.1**) as an example. This product has no pages to navigate. It's a dynamic JavaScript-based user interface, where the experience is made up of multiple features and numerous potential user journeys.

To demonstrate, let's break down the Adobe Portfolio product into a few system elements, mapped to our model:

Foundation

The example below (**FIG 4.11**) shows the brand colour palette used in the product.

FIG 4.11 Foundation example: colour palette

4.1 roomfive.net/adobe-portfolio/

Component

The following image shows a few examples of components in the product (FIG 4.12), including text inputs, checkboxes, toggles, and buttons. This is only a very limited view of a few components, and not all their states are shown, but notice the components also include things like placeholder states, hover states, and error states. We'll cover this extensively later in this book. Also, notice the only colours used are the colours we've just seen in our foundations example (FIG 4.11).

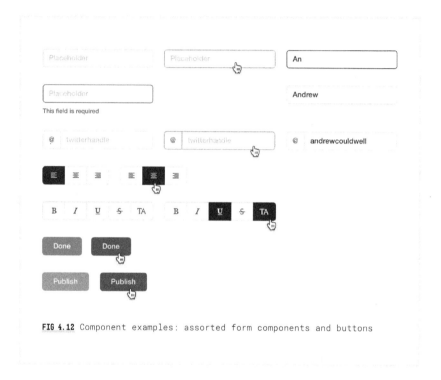

FIG 4.12 Component examples: assorted form components and buttons

Pattern

Some of the previous component examples can be seen in the following example (FIG 4.13) in a modal pattern. This example pattern is called a "Panel", which is a modal — composed mostly of components like inputs, toggles, selects, and buttons — used throughout the product as a consistent vehicle for performing various actions. The example spec shows the makeup of a Panel and a couple of variations of this pattern, including the "Basic Panel", "Advanced Panel" (with navigation), and "Manage Panel" (a fixed height panel with scrolling content).

Note: It's good practice to name your patterns. For example, our Panel pattern's technical name is a "modal", but you may find additional use cases for using a modal throughout a product, such as for warnings or messaging. It's far more efficient to say "Basic Panel" or "Advanced Panel" in a product discussion, a GitHub Issue, or a conversation with a developer, than it is to attempt to describe it: *"The modal". "Which one?". "The one with the navigation".* Instead, give it a name, document it, and use that name going forward. Over time people on your team will identify patterns by name, and if not, your documentation is where they look to find their answer. *Don't worry, we'll cover documentation later in this book.*

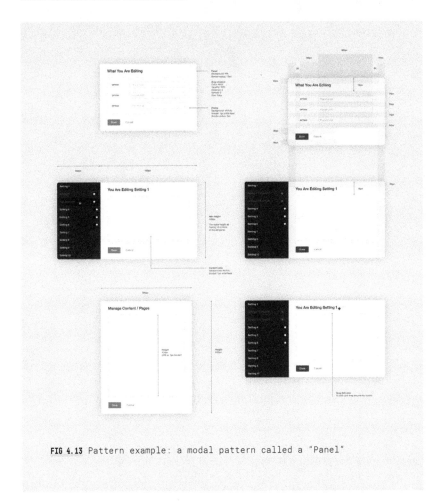

FIG 4.13 Pattern example: a modal pattern called a "Panel"

Feature

The big difference between a pattern and a feature is their complexity. A pattern might perform one or two functions, and can be deployed in a number of different ways as a reusable element. A feature can perform many functions or one specific function, and may be comprised of multiple patterns.

The example below **(FIG 4.14)** is a spec for the "Manage Content" feature from the Adobe Portfolio product, which uses the "Manage Panel" pattern **(FIG 4.13)** from our previous example. In this case, the feature is made up of many foundations and components, but is using just one pattern.

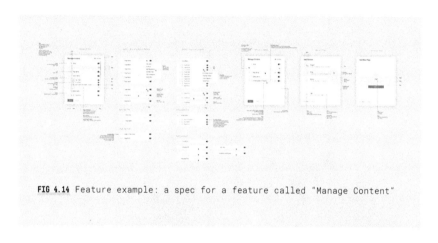

FIG 4.14 Feature example: a spec for a feature called "Manage Content"

Interaction wise, there are many things that can be done with this "Manage Content" feature. Contained within the "Panel" pattern, you can drag and drop elements, toggle things off and on, access menus, add content, delete content, edit content, and so on. These specifications (or — as I call them — 'specs' for short) map out those different interactions and states.

Note: You've seen in the previous three examples — for features, patterns, and components — that I've designed and created specifications for all the various states and interactions. We will cover this extensively throughout this book, but for now, some friendly words of advice:

Web and product designers often fail to mock up different states of components and patterns or to fully consider the interactions, pitfalls, and potential user journeys of the products they design. For example, designers will often hand over mockups of a form without showing how an input should look if there's an error, or what the submit button looks like on-hover, or what happens once the form has been submitted? I say this as a designer who's worked with other designers who are guilty of this, and as a frustrated developer who has built websites (that someone else designed) where these things haven't been considered or accounted for.

Don't assume the developers will figure it out. It's not their job, it's the designer's job. And especially don't leave it to chance, and risk later finding out your customers are struggling to use your product. This ambiguity leads to frustration, confusion, and inconsistencies in the build and user experience.

Screen

A "screen" really highlights the difference between designing a digital product and a website. Websites (often) have a definitive set of pages, and we know what they will look like as they are either based on a template or are a bespoke design. Products, on the other hand, can have dynamically created content, built up of features that are tailored to the user.

FIG 4.15 Screen example: a product scenario mockup

The Adobe Portfolio product we've been reviewing in this case study has no "pages". It's a product that people use to build personal portfolio websites for their work. No two "screens" will ever look the same — they are unique to the person using the product. But from a product design perspective, it's still valuable to visualise what those screens could look like in order to stress test and design for all variables; this also allows us to give the developers a better idea of what they're building (in addition to our design system elements and specs).

A screen is the culmination of all your foundations, components, patterns, and features coming together. It's a snapshot in time of someone using your product, or a step in their user journey.

The image **(FIG 4.15)** is a design mockup simulating a feature in use — in this case, a "Colour Picker" pattern is being used to edit a "Masthead" feature of the product. This is different from a traditional mockup or "page" design in web design, as it's only showing a pattern in the context of one part of a user's journey. Still, it's a useful way of depicting how your system elements will come together in the product.

User journey

A user journey, strictly speaking, is not part of our design system model. But, as stated before, a good product designer should map out how a product — or a feature of the product — could be used. There are many ways you can visually convey user journeys and the specific steps a user can take. You could, for example:

- Build a basic prototype you can test for real.
- Simulate interactions in an interactive prototype using design software.
- Create a still image step-by-step simulation of the product in action.
- Map out all the potential actions a user could take in a decision tree diagram or flow chart.
- Design a detailed, annotated specification showing all interactions and states, similar to the examples shown here **(FIG 4.16 - 4.18)**.

The following design mockup **(FIG 4.16)** maps out the user journey for the "Background Image" feature of the Adobe Portfolio product, which uses the "Basic Panel" pattern **(FIG 4.13)** we saw in our earlier example.

Similarly, **FIG 4.17** maps out the various steps to using the "Add Content" feature, which uses the "Manage Panel" pattern **(FIG 4.13)**.

And finally, **FIG 4.18** maps out the potential steps a user could take while using a different feature of the product, this time using the "Advanced Panel" pattern **(FIG 4.13)**.

It's my hope that seeing how the elements of the Foundations Model came together in the Adobe Portfolio product design gave you a sense for how you

FIG 4.16 User journey example: a spec showing potential user steps

FIG 4.17 Annotations help to identify what's what

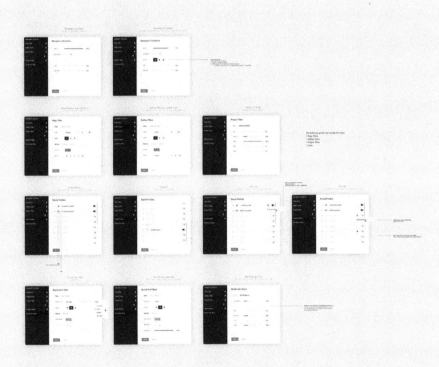

FIG 4.18 Map out the interactions and steps a user could take

can adapt the model to your project. Keep in mind, you can always adapt the model to make it yours, this is just a guide to get you started.

Allow for flexibility

A really great design system is flexible enough to have room for creativity, and be effectively applied to different scenarios. The more rigid the system, the more likely designers are to introduce rogue elements. This is a slippery slope towards the system failing, and the surest path to designers and developers falling out.

It's also healthy to think of and use terminology like 'guidelines', as opposed to 'rules'. Rules feel like laws that can't be broken. Your average designer won't like working under these constraints, so it's important your system is adaptable and leaves room for creativity.

However, some system elements do benefit from being more rigid for the sake of consistency, ease of navigation, user experience, or to protect the brand. For example, on most websites, patterns like a 'global navigation' or 'footer' will likely never change as you navigate page-to-page — nor should they, as it can be disruptive to the user journey and experience. Similarly, a 'related items' pattern in an e-commerce product, or 'related posts' in a blog will be the same design on every page (only the content changes). And foundations wise, sticking to a set of defined text styles and colours will make for a more coherent end product and experience.

It's also beneficial for some system elements to be adaptable — or to have multiple variations — to cover different scenarios. This flexibility or

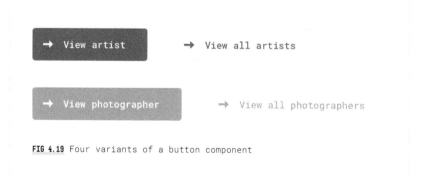

FIG 4.19 Four variants of a button component

adaptability cuts down on the need to bypass the system or go rogue, adding new elements.

For example, a component like a button could come in a small and large size, in multiple colours, or have a solid background versus a border outline to communicate different actions or hierarchy of importance.

FIG 4.19 is an example of different buttons from the same design system. While different, they clearly belong to the same (brand) family and share similar specifications and foundational characteristics.

Similarly, a component like a select could have a multi-select variant to cover scenarios where the user can select one or multiple options, as demonstrated in **FIG 4.20**.

FIG 4.20 Two variants of a select component

Document the why, when, and how

We'll cover documentation more thoroughly later in this book, but for now, it's important to state: you should document guidelines, specifications, and use cases for all your foundations, components, patterns, templates, and features.

Design system documentation acts as a **source of truth.** By documenting the design thinking behind each element, you leave nothing to assumption or misinterpretation. Demonstrating use cases is also great for guidance, as well as on-boarding new team members. Seeing is believing, so lead by example and show your team the thinking that went into your design choices.

Better together

Everything we've covered in this chapter highlights the importance of teamwork, communication, and not designing or building anything in isolation — from the terminology we use, to creating and iterating on the system elements, to documenting how, when, and why they're used.

My hope is that with the Foundations Model as a guide, you'll now have a simple framework to kickstart a great design system with your team.

Now that we're all on the same page regarding the model and terminology we'll use going forward, we're (almost) ready to start creating a design system.

The first app I
opened when we
started wasn't
Sketch. It was Google
Docs. You need to
clearly articulate
the problems you're
solving first.

GETT—ING STAR—TED

05

By now, hopefully, you should understand the importance of getting your whole team excited about the value of a design system, and involving everyone in the process.

We're not ready to jump into design just yet. First, you (and your team) need to be clear about what your goals for creating a design system are. By doing this, you are further laying the strong foundations needed to build a successful design system and product(s).

Start by identifying the problems

Much of design is problem-solving. So, first things first, you and your team need to investigate: what problems are you solving?

As tempting as it is to see design systems as a vanity project, your goal isn't — or shouldn't be, entirely — to create something beautiful. If you get everything else right, you will probably end up with something beautiful, but don't race to the finish line — it's more of a marathon than a sprint. Creating a design system is a large investment of time, by a lot of people, so you need a good set of reasons for doing it. And those reasons (or problems) will help you identify a way forward, your priorities, and which approach to creating a design system is best for your company, product, and team.

Consider this quote from Nick Stamas (**5.1**), my former colleague I mentioned in the "Selling a Design System" chapter of this book, as he reflected on the beginning of a journey that led to creating a design system:

> *"The first app I opened when we started wasn't Sketch. It was Google Docs. You need to clearly articulate the problems first. Be specific. Where are things breaking down? Where are the biggest pain points? A design system doesn't exist in a vacuum, it needs to solve problems for everyone."*

Start by involving your whole team — designers, developers, and product managers — in an open and frank discussion about where people feel the product or the team's processes are going wrong. Depending on the size of your team, and locations of the people working on your product(s), you could get everybody together, or break into smaller groups, and have team leaders

5.1 nickstamas.com

meet to discuss their findings. Document everything you discuss in a Google Doc (or something similar), so you can easily share it with the whole group.

System design is a team effort, so work as a team. Make everyone feel like their opinion is important, and their voice is heard. The easiest way to get people to believe in the system is to involve them.

When you discuss your problems as a team, you'll also have a better understanding of the extent of the work that needs to be done. You may find you already have the basis of a design system that's just gone a little astray over time, and it may not require much work to consolidate the design and code, document it, and grow from there.

A designer might look at a problem and think: *"we're screwed, let's just start again!"*, but a developer might look at the same problem and think: *"actually, if we do X then we'll be okay"*. And vice versa. This is why it's valuable to get everyone's perspective.

The goal here, ultimately, is to find the common pain points in everything from the product, design and build processes, team culture, and user feedback.

For example, some broader takeaways from this discussion could be things like:

- Developers hate it when designers reinvent the wheel.
- Product managers want to ship updates and new features faster.
- Designers are sick of the build not looking like their mockups.
- Our users are frustrated by X, Y, Z.

You're probably familiar with at least one of these frustrations... It's pretty common stuff, and all issues that design systems can help fix.

More specific takeaways could be things like:

- Why do we have 13 different colours in the product?
- We want to explore a better way of doing X.
- How can we improve conversion on this form?
- We need a consistent set of buttons.
- Our icons have no consistent style.
- We want to clear time to refactor the code.
- We want to introduce more animation in the product.
- We need a consistent set of design components to work with.

Once you know what the problems are, you're better prepared to come up with a plan of attack for solving them.

Note: Much of the above pre-supposes you're working on an existing product. But even if you're launching a brand new company or product, it's still worth identifying what you want to achieve, and the problems your product and design system aims to address. Also, identifying within your team the problems that people have faced in the past — and the potential issues that could arise going forward — can provide valuable insights you can use to set your new work up for success.

Where do we go from here?

The multi-million dollar question! There's no one-size-fits-all solution. Now you've identified the problems, you have to decide what to do about them. Chances are, if you're having discussions like this in the first place, you've more or less already decided — you're going to create a design system. Now, the harder part is deciding how to go about it.

Looking at this simplistically, there are two approaches you can take:

1. The iterative approach
2. The wholesale approach

The next two chapters are dedicated to these approaches, but before we go into detail about the process for each, I want to explain in brief what they are.

The iterative approach

The iterative approach is the process of gradually replacing what you have now with a new system. Or, if this is a new product, it's the process of launching the product in stages (i.e. more of a soft launch, as opposed to a hard launch). If you are working on an existing product, this could mean consolidating what you have currently, then gradually replacing what you have with something new. This process happens iteratively — so foundation by foundation, component by component, pattern by pattern, feature by feature, template by template, and so on.

Remember back in the chapter on "Laying the Foundations" when I talked about creating a scaffolding and gradually remodeling, as opposed to demolishing what you have and starting from scratch? That's what you're doing with an iterative approach.

An iterative
approach might
only bring small
wins at first — but a
small win can make
a huge difference
to a product's user
experience, and your
team culture.

With this approach, you start by conducting visual and code audits *(we'll cover this in the next chapter)* to discover the problem areas, and iteratively fix them. You focus on small areas of the product at a time, gradually working your way through the whole product — designing, building, and documenting a design system as you go.

This approach can be disruptive to the product's user experience and aesthetic, but less disruptive to your business and roadmap. It can also be a frustrating process, as progress can be slow.

The advantage to the iterative approach is that you're able to start small and tackle your biggest pain points first. This might bring some immediate relief to a more immediate problem, such as a user experience problem, a process problem, or a sticking point for designers and developers on your team.

Starting with the iterative approach might only bring small wins at first — but a small win can make a huge difference to a product's user experience, and your team culture. A positive start can have a profound impact on an organisation's positivity towards — and belief in — a design system as a worthwhile investment of their time going forward. This proved effective at GitHub **(5.2)**, who said of their design system process:

> *"Tackling our biggest pain points and working on tasks that provided high value to designers and developers, helped us start to build recognition and show the value of design systems."*

We'll delve more into the iterative approach in the next chapter, but for now it's worth considering if this might be the best way for your team to start creating a design system. Alternatively, you could try:

The wholesale approach

The wholesale approach is essentially starting from scratch — either because you're designing a new product without any existing systems in place, or because you've decided to tear down what you have and start again.

Taking a wrecking ball to your existing design is arguably a more extreme option, but it has its advantages. You avoid the potential 'Frankenstein Monster problem' of the iterative approach, which could protect your brand

---

5.2 medium.com/@broccolini/design-systems-at-github-c8e5378d2542

and user experience. Changes will be widespread and coherent, as opposed to the 'bitty' experience that can happen when things are tweaked iteratively. Also, you'll ultimately launch with a beautiful new product, which could be a great marketing opportunity!

However, a big undertaking like this could be more disruptive to your business. It's likely any roadmap of new feature releases or improvements will more or less be put on hold while you undertake a redesign. This is why it's important to involve product managers and other business stakeholders in design system talks, as well as designers and developers. For example, someone outside the design and development teams could easily say: *"if it ain't broke, don't fix it"* — so to sell them on a wholesale redesign, you'll need to convince them of just how broken things are.

If you're considering condemning your current design and building something new, be prepared to answer the following questions:

- Will redesigning solve a business problem?
- Has your research shown that your users are unhappy?
- Is your product underperforming on certain metrics?
- Are you rebranding to reach a new audience?
- Does your brand need to evolve in line with its growth?
- *Or are your designers just bored? (Joking, not joking).*

Be smart about which approach you choose

A totally new design might look great in your portfolio, a Medium article, or a Dribbble post, but it might also have a negative affect on your business. Your customers come first, so don't lose sight of what affect your new design system might have on their behaviour and their retention.

Think about websites like Amazon, which has largely looked the same for years. Given their enormous wealth, one would think they could easily afford a huge wholesale redesign. Instead, Amazon employs more of an iterative approach. They refine and test different design changes over time. Their product and design system evolves, but the user doesn't always notice. There's a very good reason why companies like Amazon don't take a wholesale approach, as the unknown factor of how their customers will respond to a radical redesign is far too great a risk.

5.3 vanityfair.com/news/2018/05/snapchat-publishers-discover-redesign

A wholesale redesign is a gamble — it could make or break your business. Take Snapchat's 2018 redesign, which Vanity Fair described as "cataclysmic" (5.3). More than 1.25 million people signed a petition urging Snap to undo their update, they lost 2% of their daily active users (some 3 million users), and their stock price bombed! *I can only imagine how bad those days were for their product teams.*

The risk of taking the wholesale approach is especially high for e-commerce websites and digital consumer products that people frequently use; it's less of an issue for marketing based websites or products with lower repeat visitors. Humans are creatures of habit — we don't always like change.

An iterative approach is less disruptive and therefore can be safer, but sometimes a wholesale brand refresh can have a positive effect — look at brands like Airbnb, whose new design system and accompanying redesign *(circa 2016?)* set a new standard for iOS app design, and helped them continue to grow as a successful business. You need to weigh up your options, and their potential risks and rewards.

Choices, choices

It very much depends on the size and complexity of your product, team, and audience — as well as the nature of your brand — as to which approach is better, more expensive, disruptive, time-consuming, or worthwhile.

Both approaches divert from business-as-usual tasks. While an iterative approach can be undertaken largely under the radar and requires less stakeholder support, a wholesale approach will require more serious buy-in from multiple stakeholders, as it will suck up a lot of resources, and arguably carries greater risk.

As you read through the following two chapters — delving more into each of the iterative and wholesale approaches — you'll no doubt conclude there are common elements to both, and you'd be correct. The word "holistic" is an important theme and consideration in both approaches, which we'll explore. The answer for your company might not be to adopt one approach or the other, but to apply lessons from both approaches. In fact, I would recommend doing a mix of the two!

Let's start by looking at the iterative approach.

AN ITER— ATIVE APP— ROACH

06

With this approach, you start by conducting visual and code audits to discover the problem areas. Next, focus on small areas of the product at a time, gradually working your way through the whole product — re-designing, building, and documenting a design system as you go.

While this is more of a piecemeal approach, it is still important to not lose sight of the design holistically — to consider how everything will work together.

Find your team

You're not going to get far on your own. Find designers who are excited about making the best product! Find engineers who seem most excited about the idea of a system — or the front-end code — and make them your new best friends!

In 2017, at a design system meetup in New York City, I watched as Diana Mounter (6.1) — a design system lead at GitHub — talked about how in the early days of creating the Primer design system (6.2), they formed a small task force who met regularly to discuss, discover, and plan to solve problem areas. They reviewed code. They took action on making incremental improvements, consolidating their system, and making the system more accessible to their design team.

Diana's article, *Design Systems at GitHub* (6.3), is an excellent insight into design systems:

> "There weren't obvious underlying systems connecting all the pieces together. I knew things could be better and I was enthusiastic about making improvements — I quickly discovered I wasn't the only one that felt this way. There were several folks working on efforts to improve things, but weren't working together. With support from design leads, a group of us started to meet regularly to discuss improvements and prioritize work — this was the beginning of the design systems team."

6.1 broccolini.net

6.2 primer.style/css

6.3 medium.com/@broccolini/design-systems-at-github-c8e5378d2542

Once you've found your team: a good way to get going is to conduct interface audits.

Interface audits

'Interface audit' is a term with potentially different definitions. So for the sake of clarity — in this book — consider that:

- An 'interface audit' is a broad term for conducting audits on a digital product.
- A 'visual audit' is a design-based audit of what you can see in a digital product, focussed on foundations, components, and patterns.
- You could focus the scope of a visual audit, and do only a 'pattern audit' or a 'component audit'.
- A 'code audit' is an audit of what you can't see, but what makes everything work behind the scenes: CSS, HTML, JavaScript, and so on.
- A 'colour audit' takes stock of colours used across all digital properties.
- A 'content audit' maps out what you're communicating and where.

Essentially, an 'audit' is whatever you need it to be. It's an investigation, and a great starting point that leads to larger discussions, actions, or projects.

Colour audits

You might be surprised by how many rogue colours you have in your product, but the good news is, this is one of the simplest things to action.

First, you need to do a colour audit of all websites and products at your company. Take note of every unique colour used for text, links, backgrounds, form inputs, buttons, error states, borders, and so on. If you have more than one website, create a different colour palette for each website — it might prove interesting to see the comparison.

As an extreme example, a colour audit conducted by Hipmunk **(6.4)** discovered an alarming amount of colours used in their product.

6.4 uxdesign.cc/hipmunk-design-system-part-1-colors-ux-case-study-1ac99806aabd

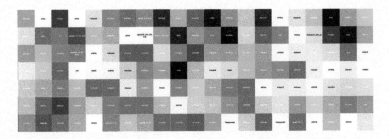

FIG 6.1 Colour audit of Hipmunk's product

Their colour audit **(FIG 6.1)** led to them creating a stripped-down, clearer, and on-brand semantic colour system **(FIG 6.2)**:

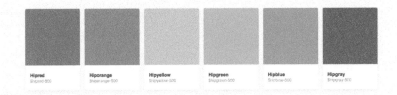

| Hipred | Hiporange | Hipyellow | Hipgreen | Hipblue | Hipgray |
| $hipred-500 | $hiporange-500 | $hipyellow-500 | $hipgreen-500 | $hipblue-500 | $hipgray-500 |

FIG 6.2 Hipmunk's new colour palette created post-audit

Note the use of the number "500" (e.g. $hipred-500) in Hipmunk's new colour palette (above). We'll come back to what this means and why it's important in the "Systematising the Design" chapter, when we cover naming conventions and creating colour systems.

The following example **(FIG 6.3)** is a small sample from a real colour audit I conducted at a company. The example colours shown here are to demonstrate the discrepancies, which in this case were very similar variants of the same colours.

FIG 6.3 Colour audit reveals very similar colours used

Once you have your audit results — you need to get to the bottom of:

- Why are we using each colour?
- What (if any) function does each colour provide?
- Do we need multiple variants of the same colour?
- Which colours can we safely remove, and what do we replace them with?

It's wise to take stock of **why** a colour is used. Consider whether the colours you find in an audit were used intentionally (and serve an important function), or whether they were used unintentionally (and can be changed).

When we clean our example up — removing the rogue colours — we end up with a condensed, on-brand colour palette like so **(FIG 6.4)**:

FIG 6.4 New on-brand colour palette removing unnecessary colours

Now you need to work with a front-end developer to make these changes in the code. If you're working with a website, this is the perfect opportunity to introduce Sass variables for colours (work with a developer for this). Create Sass variables for all the correct brand colours you've defined, paying attention to how you name the colours.

We'll cover naming conventions and why replacing static hex values (e.g. #F00658) in your code with Sass variables is a good idea later in the "Systematising the Design" chapter.

Finally, pair a designer with a developer and go through the website, replacing all hex value colours with the correct Sass variable (colour). You could do a 'fast and dirty' find and replace, but it's probably safer to 'eyeball it', going page-by-page and scenario-by-scenario.

Code audits

We're not going to go too deep into code audits in this book since we're focussed more on design, but suffice it to say they are important. The efficiency of the code is key to a design system's success — and to the ease, speed, efficiency, consistency, maintenance, and scalability of a digital product.

Sometimes, the code harbours many of the problems. If you've worked in-house at a company with any history of digital, you've no doubt come across the phrase 'legacy problems'. This often refers to legacy (old) code that makes updating something problematic *(read: painful)*. The problems may stem from design — perhaps designers have gone rogue designing several variants of the same thing — but the code holds the key to fixing them. Refactoring the code (reducing complexity) makes all the difference, and a code audit is a great way to kickstart that refactoring effort.

At GitHub, their designers and developers worked together to audit **(6.5)**, refactor, and consolidate their design system, focussing on their code:

> *"We reduced the need for people to have to write new CSS. We made our components easier to reuse in multiple locations. We worked on consolidating patterns by reducing code repetition and removing unnecessary design variations. We defined global Sass variables for shared system styles. We introduced consistent and easy-to-internalize naming conventions."*

"Sass" is a key word here. If you're not already familiar with it, Google it. Speak to your developers about it. It's a way of writing and compiling CSS that will make your code much easier to manage.

Besides the code, I even introduced Sass naming conventions into the design and design documentation at a previous job — bridging the gap between

---

6.5 medium.com/@broccolini/design-systems-at-github-c8e5378d2542

design and engineering. Any way you can find to do this is a good idea. We'll cover this later in the "Systematising the Design" chapter.

Experience has taught me that visual audits and their resulting plans of action, often dovetail into or spur subsequent code audits in the execution to fix the visual problem. Your teams might divide and conquer — running both visual and code audits simultaneously — or start with one or the other, and work from there. It very much depends on the nature of your teams and the problems you're solving.

Visual audits

A visual audit (aka 'interface inventory') is a means of finding inconsistencies in a digital product. You scan through a product and create an inventory of all aspects of the visual interface, identifying where the problems are, and scoping out the extent of the problem.

With this information, you can plan to fix any smaller issues in the short term, and formulate plans for fixing larger issues in the long term.

They also provide you with excellent material to sell your design system work to stakeholders — referring back to the "Selling a Design System" chapter — since they highlight why you need a design system!

How do you conduct a visual audit?

This can easily be a one-person job, but I would recommend using this as an awareness and 'togetherness' exercise by working as a group.

Create a small task force of people who care most about the front-end. The team could all be designers, or you could involve developers and product managers as well (so long as they are more 'visually oriented' people — it's important they take the audit seriously, so nothing slips through the cracks).

Call a meeting and introduce the audit as an exercise to find inconsistencies in your product, which will ultimately help you to design and build a more consistent product.

Start by creating a list of every feature, page, screen, user journey, and scenario in your product. Then divide that list up amongst the group, with each person taking ownership for their part of the product(s)/audit.

Agree on a place to store your findings. It should be accessible by everyone; I recommend a Google Doc or a design tool like Sketch, but there are a number of online collaboration tools you could use. You could also use something like Keynote. It will be easier if you agree on a consistent format for cataloguing and organising your findings. Ideally, create a template for your team to use.

The task of each auditor is to document what they see. So for every page, screen, or user journey: take a screenshot of each button, header style, text style, link, form input, toggle, pagination, tooltip, quote, product card, table, header, footer, navigation, and so on — and organise them by category (e.g. buttons, text links, header styles, etc.).

The goal here is not to capture (screenshot) every instance of an element, but to **capture each unique variant** of it. So, don't capture 10 instances of the exact same header style. Instead, if you find that 4 of those 10 header styles are a different font family, weight, size, colour, sentence case versus title case, all caps, or underlined — then capture each of those variants. Do the same for all foundations, components, and patterns. Pay close attention to things like size, spacing, colour, text styling, border-radius, drop-shadows, and icons. And don't forget things like hover states and error states.

Organisation is key. For example, you want to end up with a view of how many button styles you have in your product, but it may also help to know where in the product you found each button style, so you can go back and address it later.

You should end up with a mass inventory of all existing foundations, components, and patterns in your product, and all of their variations.

Finally, schedule a time to meet again at a later date, as a group, to share and discuss what the team found.

The results may shock you

If you're shocked, this is a good thing. The first step towards solving a problem is admitting (or seeing) there is a problem. Chances are you've already done that by forming this task force in the first place. You're aware of the inconsistencies in your product, and you want to prove to others that they exist. The audit(s) will uncover these inconsistencies — and that's only the surface layer, what lies beneath (aka the code) may well be a lot worse!

Seeing the number of variations side-by-side is a powerful realisation of the state of your product, and an indication of how much work lies ahead. A visual audit can help recruit people to your cause, convince stakeholders that something needs to be done, and acts as a blueprint to create a design system.

Web developer/designer, Brad Frost **(6.6)** puts it well:

> *"It's not to say that deviating from established patterns is always a bad idea, but it's important to recognize the difference between intentional and unintentional deviation. An interface inventory helps expose unintentional inconsistencies and encourages consistent, deliberate design decisions."*

What now?

Now, your team needs to plan what to do about the inconsistencies you've found.

Interface audits are a valuable addition to your pitch to stakeholders for why you need to invest in a design system. As I said before, seeing is believing. You can show your stakeholders the extent of the problem, and explain why these inconsistencies matter, or you can take a more direct approach, and take action now.

Principally you need to work with your task force to consolidate the variations you found. By task force, I mean: designers and developers working together to fix the inconsistencies, and documenting the definitive solutions you decide upon.

This is where it helps to include front-end developers in your task force, or at least bring them into the fold once you've completed the visual audit. You won't get far without developers, or at least not without access to the code to make the changes yourself *(yes, I'm suggesting designers could write code).*

Research, consolidate, and document

A visual audit I was once a part of uncovered 26 different styles of buttons in a single product. A subsequent code audit revealed an array of different classes, colour variations, and naming conventions for the same and similar buttons. It was a mess.

6.6 bradfrost.com

The goal is not to just eradicate all the variations you find. You need to replace them with something, and the answer might not be to replace 26 with 1. In this case, we dug a little deeper into the audit, analysing the 26 styles of buttons; we asked ourselves:

- Are the variants random, or intentional?
- Where, when, and how are they used?
- What are their different functions?

Chances are you'll find more than one use of the component, but I'll wager you won't find more than a few. Trending patterns will emerge. Actions like: 'Save', 'Submit', 'Get Started', 'Sign Up', 'Buy Now', and 'Subscribe' may differ in function, prominence, or importance from actions like: 'Edit', 'Cancel', 'Read More', and 'Close'. Take stock of these different functions in your audits and decision-making.

Your visual audit helps you to uncover not only how many variants you have, but potentially *why* you have those variations. Sometimes it's just bad design, or proof for why you need a design system. Other times you'll discover a legitimate need for variations — like multiple button styles for different actions, or additional text styles to cover specific scenarios.

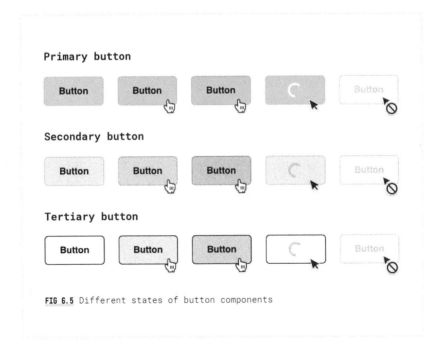

FIG 6.5 Different states of button components

Now that you've uncovered and debated these findings, you can consolidate those 26 button styles into 1, 2, 3, or more styles that cover all the scenarios you've identified. Ending up with something like this **(FIG 6.5)**.

Note the naming conventions. Names like "Primary", "Secondary", and "Tertiary" (for example), make it easier to identify your defined system components — keeping everyone on the same page and speaking the same language. Your naming conventions should be consistently used in the design, code, documentation, and any product discussions.

The documentation should also specify why you have these variations:

How, where, when, and why should you use each variant?

The code should also be documented:

How does one apply each component, and their variants, in the code?

Documentation is a source of truth that reduces the chance of these multiple rogue variations happening in the first place. We'll cover design system documentation in greater detail later in this book, but for now know it's a key step not to be overlooked.

Once you've consolidated, designed, and documented your component — work with a developer to build your new component and all its variants. And once it's built you'll need to work through the product and replace all the rogue variants with your new, consistent component. Your audit might help you to do this if you've already identified where they occur in the product.

Managing the workload

Now, let's not kid ourselves... The iterative approach will no doubt be executed over a great period of time — working in sprints — but, ultimately, it will be worth the wait.

If you're not familiar with sprints: it's common practice for in-house design and development teams to work in short pre-defined sprints, focussing on completing a limited (achievable) number of tasks in each sprint. Some companies even group their sprints by quarter (of the year), aiming to achieve specific goals at key stages throughout the year. Sprint and quarterly achievements can be good for keeping tabs on, encouraging, and reporting the progress of your design system, which helps to keep stakeholders happy.

One of the advantages of the iterative approach is that it can be done alongside business-as-usual tasks. I recommend advocating for allotting a certain percentage of time in each sprint to focus on the design system. If you've done a good job selling the system, advocating for its importance, and gaining support from product managers, developers, and designers, then this should be no issue.

The order in which you approach the system — iteratively — is unique to your situation.

You could **focus by order of importance**. For example, focus on a problem area based on its affect on the user experience, the severity of the problem it's solving, or even its impact on your team's happiness or productivity! Tackling the system by order of importance can be smart, as you (or rather, your stakeholders) might see a more immediate impact — gaining your design system more support and traction.

Or you could **focus by level of disruption**. For example, introducing foundational elements like colours and text styles will likely be less disruptive than, say, introducing a new pattern that's more noticeably different from its surrounding patterns. I advise starting small with colours and text styles, then move up in scale and disruption (i.e. noticeability by the user) to components like buttons and inputs, and eventually to larger patterns like navigation, cards, galleries, footer, and so on.

In time your product will gradually morph into a new look product, powered by a design system.

The Frankenstein monster effect

While designing iteratively has many advantages, it's easy to lose sight of the product or brand as a whole. Without careful management, it can lead to an unfortunate 'Frankenstein monster' effect.

Let's step back for a second. It's not as simple as just taking an 'iterative' or a 'wholesale' approach. You must consider the design and brand as a whole, coherent piece. A system without harmony isn't much of a system.

A jigsaw puzzle starts as a whole picture before it's broken down into pieces. You'd have a terrible puzzle if you designed the pieces first, then later discovered they don't fit together!

Don't create design system elements in isolation, then attempt to fit them together in a product. Think about the product as a whole — as an experience.

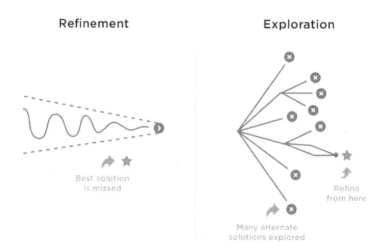

Refinement   Exploration

Best solution
is missed

Many alternate
solutions explored

Refine
from here

FIG 6.6 Refinement vs. exploration

6.7 intercom.com/blog/two-product-principles-often-forgotten/

Refinement vs. exploration

Based on a concept from the book, *Sketching User Experiences* by Bill Buxton
— the following graphic (FIG 6.6) beautifully illustrates a good point to keep
in mind when approaching a design system iteratively. Focussing on refining
what you have now — or changing your current design one piece at a time —
can blind you to the best solution.

When we design holistically, exploring many alternative solutions, we're more
likely to discover an optimal solution. Then we can refine from there.

To quote from an article (6.7) by Des Traynor, co-founder of Intercom:

> *"Iterating until something is 'not obviously broken' doesn't guarantee
> a good product. You can iterate your way to lots of places, including
> mediocrity."*

The iterative approach has many advantages, as we've covered in this chapter.
However, if you take the iterative approach, don't focus only on refinement,
or work with too narrow a focus. Take time to explore each problem area first,
then refine. Don't bypass the opportunity for design exploration altogether.

The wholesale approach centers more on design exploration and holistic
design. Let's look at this approach next.

A WHOLE— SALE APP— ROACH

07

The wholesale approach ideally should start in a similar way to the iterative approach we covered earlier: by identifying the problems you're trying to solve. A little user and product research wouldn't hurt either, but we can only cover so much ground in this book! So, we're going to assume that you're clued up, you've identified that a redesign would be a good move for your business, and you have a good idea of the problems you're trying to solve.

Okay, now you're ready for design exploration!

Ground your work in reality

If you're creating a design system for an existing product, then use real scenarios from that product(s). Don't design with convenient content — for example, don't design using uniformly short names, or headlines that conveniently only use four words. Use real (or realistic) content, and use unruly content too! Let's be honest, if you've been designing for awhile then you know what some clients are capable of when it comes to content. Is your beautiful, Dribbble-shot-perfect layout with a large font size and three-word headline going to work when the client adds a 10-word headline? Use unreasonably long (and short) titles. Use awkwardly lengthy words that break the width of content areas. Discover the pitfalls in your design and create something responsive that works in the real world, not just in your idealistic, perfect design mockup.

Design for all scenarios, not just the best case scenarios. Don't try to fit the content to your design. Design for the content.

If you're creating a design system for a new product with no existing content, you still have to design with content in mind. Use a close approximation, or work with a content strategist, copywriter, or user experience expert to get as close as possible to the final content you'll be using in the product.

The goal here is not to create the prettiest system, it's to design a system that best meets your product, user, and business needs. We do, of course, set out to create delightful products, but only because delight can enhance the user experience.

Have fun with it

Get your team together. Let your designers flex their muscles. Collaborate, but let your designers express their individual creativity too — *they're on your team for a reason, right?* Go far and wide. Explore every angle, style, layout, and approach for potential new design directions for your product. Be creative. Chisel away and simplify until you discover the right style, form, and function.

If you've already established Digital Foundations — as we covered in an earlier chapter — or your company has brand guidelines — then use them as a North Star, so to speak. If your company has no brand guidelines of any description, then these design explorations will help you discover, flesh out, and document your brand!

Design process, systematisation, and documentation

As you discover, refine, and arrive at a style and voice that speaks to your brand and solves problems for your product, a design system — or at least a consistent visual language — will start to emerge.

Once this consistent visual language emerges, the task now is to document the design system elements you've created, accounting for all states and scenarios. Document your design thinking. How, where, when, and why should you apply the foundations, components, and patterns you've created?

Essentially, you're creating a comprehensive style guide for your team to use. Think of it as a blueprint for designing products at your company.

For a more detailed look at the design exploration phase of the wholesale approach and its progression towards a design system, you can read my case study (7.1), which gives a detailed account of the process described here.

Building a visual language

I recommend reading an article (7.2) by Karri Saarinen (7.3), a principal designer on the Airbnb design team, titled, *Building a Visual Language*.

There are three things worth noting about Airbnb's approach. Firstly, and interestingly: the Airbnb design team use terms like: "Design Visual Language" and "Design Language System," instead of: "Design System".

A language is more than words, it's about communication. Yes, "system" and "language" essentially mean the same thing in this case, but psychologically, perhaps the term 'language' is less intimidating to a designer than 'system'?

7.1 medium.com/@andrewcouldwell/plasma-design-system-4d63fb6c1afc

7.2 airbnb.design/building-a-visual-language/

7.3 karrisaarinen.com

For whatever reason, they've decided to use terminology that works best for their team.

I think Airbnb's philosophy is a healthy one. Anyone who's travelled knows how important language is for communicating effectively and clearly, and how wrong it can go when we don't speak the same language. This is a good philosophy to bring into system design thinking. Whatever terms and naming conventions you decide to use — just make sure you're using a language your team identifies with. The more comfortable they are with it, the more successful it will be.

Secondly, to quote from the Airbnb article **(7.2)**:

> *"We started by auditing and printing out many of our designs, both old and new. Laying the flows side by side on a board, we could see where and how the experiences were breaking, and where we needed to start making changes."*

An important thing to note here is that they focussed on product flows and the user experience. They didn't focus on small, siloed areas of the interface, or component parts that make up their products. They contemplated their product as a whole, as an "experience".

Also, they used real product scenarios. Grounding your work in reality, using real data and scenarios is key. Don't work with ideals, best case scenarios, and convenient content. Work with what you've got — and design a system that works for it — but keep it flexible enough to evolve and account for more than you have now.

Our goal here is not to create the prettiest system. It's to create a flexible system that solves problems, and also delivers a great user experience.

Thirdly: remember when we talked about Digital Foundations earlier in this book? Well, Airbnb thinks about their brand and products in a similar way.

Prior to their 'Design Language System' project, Airbnb's design team had already defined their equivalent of Digital Foundations by establishing colour, typography, and spacing **(FIG 7.1)**.

Type	A11y Color	Spacing
Title 1 · 44/56	Rausch #FF5A5F 3.05:1	8 · tiny
Title 2 · 32/36	A11y Babu #00A699 3.03:1	16 · small
Title 3 · 24/28		24 · base
Large · 19/24	A11y Arches #FC642D 3.0:1	48 · large
Regular · 17/22	A11y Hof #484848 9.14:1	64 · x-large
Small · 14/18	A11y Foggy #767676 4.54:1	

FIG 7.1 Airbnb's foundations

The exercise now was to build a design system upon those foundations:

> *"The foundation proved essential for guiding our work in a unified direction while allowing room for us to individually explore creative design solutions. This way we felt that we were all working together, towards the same idea."*

This is great! Their foundations — remember: Digital Foundations are brand guidelines, not a design system in itself — helped them work better as a team, and their designers retained their individual creativity, which is very important to designers!

> *"Reviewing our collective work at the end of each day, we began to see patterns emerge. We course-corrected when necessary, and started defining our standardized components."*

Airbnb took a holistic approach to create a visual language that worked for their product. They reviewed their work as a team, and their design explorations gradually led to patterns and components emerging throughout the process — ultimately forming their design system.

The goal is not to create the prettiest system, get more likes on Dribbble, or impress your friends — it's to design a system that best meets your product, user, and business needs.

Build and launch plans

Now, the really tricky part. With your system effectively designed (with the wholesale approach), you have a hard decision to make:

1. Do you build everything behind the scenes, and launch when it's ready?
2. Or do you build and introduce the system iteratively over time?

Brands we associate with high standards for how their brand is executed — like Nike or Apple — are more likely to take the first approach. It would be damaging to their brand perception to release anything too short of the final product.

On the other hand, smaller businesses that aren't under the microscope as much as bigger brands can afford a more iterative approach, since their changes are more likely to go unnoticed, *or at least, won't light up Twitter!*

It's important to factor in whether your business can afford to — or if your customers/target audience are willing to — wait several months or a year (plus) for you to design, build, and launch a perfect end product. Time-sensitive companies like startups are less likely to have the luxury of doing months of design and build work followed by a big reveal, due to their limited funds and need to prove themselves a worthwhile and profitable company in a very short timespan. Often times — dependending on the product and industry — the smart thing to do is to get something out there, test the water, and iterate to find a market fit.

It doesn't have to be perfect

There's no one-size-fits-all approach to how you build and launch a website or digital product. You have to do what's best for your product, team, and business. And remember: it doesn't have to be perfect.

Design is a process. It takes time. However, **building the system (i.e. development) is the lion's share of the work! If you spend too long perfecting the system on the design side you'll never launch anything!**

You might not get it right the first time, so consider getting to an MVP (minimum viable product) — or a beta launch phase — as fast as possible. This way you can soft launch to a limited subset of people, discover any problems, iterate, refine, and improve before launching to everybody. Let's look at an example:

Wholesale design, and an iterative build and launch

Earlier I mentioned it isn't always as simple as taking either the iterative approach or the wholesale approach; you can combine the two. For example, when I worked at Behance **(7.4)** on the Adobe Portfolio **(7.5)** product **(FIG 7.2)** — we took a wholesale approach to the design and (most of the) build of the product, but the launch (and the remainder of the build) was iterative.

FIG 7.2 Design mockup from the Adobe Portfolio product

For context: the new Adobe Portfolio product was replacing an existing product (Behance ProSite). A decision had been made not to iteratively evolve the existing product, but to start again with a new product (i.e. a wholesale approach). There was nothing iterative about this redesign; it was very much an 'out with the old, in with the new' wholesale approach. We were creating a new code infrastructure, a new design, and a new brand.

Months of design exploration and system design work ensued before anything substantial was built. Once the design was reasonably progressed, I started feeding the developers things to build as fast as I could — starting small with

7.4 behance.net

7.5 roomfive.net/adobe-portfolio/

system components, and working up to patterns and product features.

Building and launching a product of this size and scope was never going to be easy. We knew what we were creating was ambitious, complicated, and multifaceted. On the one hand, we had a potential target audience (of millions of people) to impress and convert to paying customers. And on the other hand, we owed it to our existing product users to keep them happy while — as seamlessly as possible — transitioning them over to the new product.

Achieving the above with a 'hard launch' would probably have proven futile, especially for a company the size of Adobe. Instead, after months of build work we arrived at an MVP (minimum viable product) version of the product. It was basic, it didn't include all the features, and it was a little buggy — but it was enough to start getting valuable feedback, user testing, and bug reports.

We did several phased Beta releases of the product over time. Each release opened up the product to more people, building towards an 'official' launch some months later.

We learned a lot from this beta phase. We especially learned that people didn't always use the product the way we anticipated they would! But that's okay. It was better to learn these things in a beta phase — with hundreds/thousands of users — than later with thousands/millions of users. People were also more forgiving about the limited feature set and bugs in the product because in our marketing we set the expectation that they were using a 'work in progress' version of the product.

The disruption factor

An important factor you should consider when deciding whether to go for the 'big reveal' approach to launching a new system — versus an iterative transition — is the effect it will have on your users.

For example, think about digital productivity products you use on a daily basis... I mean meticulously use — they're mission-critical to your job. For some professions, CRM (customer relationship management) products are a great example of this kind of product. An experienced CRM product user could be so familiar with that product's user interface, they could almost operate it in their sleep. Now consider what happens when they log in one morning, and — *poof!* — there's a totally new-look product. Suddenly their day-to-day tasks aren't so easy, fast, or efficient. You could go from a satisfied user base to a frustrated one overnight (remember the Snapchat example in the "Getting Started" chapter). You might even lose those customers — considering your product likely isn't their only option.

Rolling out a design system, responsibly

Big changes to products that are used daily — or frequently — can be hugely disruptive to your customers' lives and/or businesses. Not to mention the near impossible task of managing anything that goes wrong with a large launch or update across so many touchpoints. The support requests alone would cripple some community support and product teams.

For these kinds of products (or use cases), it might be better to take it slow.

Minimise disruption to the user by subtly integrating foundations, components, and patterns in sprints. You can scale up, evolve, and improve the look and experience of a product over time — building sustainably towards the full design system integration.

Another advantage of this is that you can manage user feedback more efficiently. Feedback inline with specific system updates allows you to refine and improve on the design system in more targeted and manageable sprints, as opposed to being overwhelmed by feedback on the system at large.

The disadvantage is it can be frustrating integrating a system in stages. From a designer/developer perspective, you just want to see 'your baby' out in the world. It can feel like an eternity watching your ugly duckling slowly evolve into a swan.

The key is not to cause too much frustration at the user's end. In any form of design: **meeting people's basic expectations will keep them satisfied, and delighting them is an experience to strive for**. It's crucial to get the basics right. That's what your users care most about. Keep this in mind when rolling out your design system.

Now that you've learned the pros and cons of the wholesale and iterative approaches, you can make a more informed decision about the most suitable plan of attack for creating and deploying a design system at your company. Do you take:

- A wholesale approach to the design, build, and launch?
- An iterative approach to the design, build, and launch?
- A wholesale approach to the design, then iteratively build and launch?
- A wholesale approach to the design and build, then iteratively launch?

Whichever path(s) you go down for creating your product(s) and brand's visual language, you don't want all that hard work to go to waste. You need to safeguard the design decisions you've made, and put systems and processes in place to protect the brand and visual language you've created. The next couple of chapters teach you how to do just that. We'll also cover how to level up as designers and design teams by systematising our designs, and creating robust, efficient, accessible, and scalable design systems!

A jigsaw puzzle starts as a whole picture before it's broken down into pieces. You'd have a terrible puzzle if you designed the pieces first, then later discovered they don't fit together!

SYS— TEMAT— ISING THE DESIGN

08

Designing and building a design system is all very well and good, but your design team's continued adoption of the system is the key to its success.

It's important your design team:

1. Can easily access and design with it.
2. Understand how to design with it.
3. Maintain and iterate on it (i.e. the design and code stay in sync).

We'll look at points 2 and 3 in later chapters. In this chapter, we'll focus on point 1: Ease of access and use.

Set the system up for success

All the design exploration, pretty style guides, Digital Foundations, documentation, and goodwill in the world won't help unless your design team actually uses your design system and doesn't fight it.

I've seen this first-hand: there's a design system in place, yet individuals on a design team continue to serve up new text styles, buttons, and inputs in their mockups. It's frustrating. It creates unrest in the team. Developers get frustrated that designers still aren't using consistent components. And the system gradually falls into decay.

Sometimes, there are legitimate reasons to introduce new styles, or new variants on existing foundations, components, patterns, templates, or features. We call this '**intentional** design', and it's fine, as long as you document the system changes accordingly. But the problem I'm talking about comes from '**unintentional** design'.

Let's give the designer who introduces new system elements the benefit of the doubt. Perhaps they didn't mean to create a new image gallery when there's already a perfectly good image gallery designed, built, and ready to deploy.

1. Perhaps they unintentionally deviated from the established pattern.
2. Perhaps they're proposing adding a conditional variation to the pattern.
3. Or perhaps they are proposing a new and improved pattern.

If it's the latter (2 or 3), you should discuss the proposed iteration as a team. If it's the former (1), then you have a problem. An avoidable problem.

You need a design system library

If your design system foundations, components, and patterns are easy to access and use, you'll be less likely to have the problem of unintentional design. Think of this collection of design system assets as your 'design library'.

Here's a quote from the Airbnb design team (**8.1**) talking about their design library:

> *"We collected them [design system components] in a master file called the library, which we referred to throughout the design process. After a week or two, we began to see huge leaps in productivity by using the library when iterating on designs. One day, while putting together a last-minute prototype, our team was able to create nearly 50 screens within just a few hours by using the framework our library provided."*

I've seen designers create buttons by drawing a rectangle, changing the colour, adding a border-radius, adding some text, and styling the text how they feel like it. They do the same for text input, selects, and so on. The developers build the design mockup they're given, creating new, one-off components and non-reusable CSS each time. Is it any wonder some websites and products have so many different styles when designers work like this? There is a better way.

If this were a presentation, I'd now do a live demo. I'd open up a blank Sketch canvas and create a simple form in a matter of seconds by using an example library of design system components. Anytime I've done this it's wowed the audience. But this is no magic trick — it's just good design system management.

By creating a library of things like text styles, colours, form inputs, and buttons — that anyone on your team can easily access and use in their designs — you reduce the likelihood of unintentional design.

Ultimately, your aim is to create a master design system ("library") file — or source of truth — that your whole team can easily access and sync any updates made to it. This file (or whatever form it takes) becomes your design library.

The library should contain **reusable** elements from your design system that

8.1 airbnb.design/building-a-visual-language/

After a week or two we saw huge leaps in productivity by using the library when iterating on designs. One day our team was able to create nearly 50 screens within just a few hours.

you commonly use in your design mockups, such as text styles, form inputs, and buttons. It should also include all their **variations** and **states** (e.g. a text input's placeholder, value, hover, error, and disabled states).

Ideally, any changes you make to the master design library file should sync to your design files, keeping your design mockups in sync with the system. It's not perfect, but you're essentially trying to simulate a built environment (e.g. Sass, CSS, HTML, JS, React) in a design tool.

The idea is your design team can insert any of these elements into their design mockups. Of course these elements need to be editable, but within consistent parameters. For example, if you have two buttons in your design system — a blue button and a green button — the designer should easily be able to choose between blue and green, but not make it pink. The data/text content/value also needs to be editable, which means your components need to be **responsive** so they will work with variable amounts of content.

Constraints are not a bad thing

When we talk about using design libraries, we are essentially talking about setting 'constraints' for designers, but this shouldn't be viewed as a negative.

Pre-made components and pre-defined text styles only help designers do their job. It's important that designers on your team understand this, and don't view design systems as taking away — or restricting — their creative freedom.

For example, you can design something like a form very quickly — even in seconds — using a library of pre-made components like inputs, selects, radio buttons, and buttons. This is much faster than meticulously creating each component from scratch (risking unintentional variations), or copying and pasting components from one design file to another.

The constraints a design library puts in place help maintain consistency, and vastly increases speed and efficiency.

Freeing designers from re-creating the same foundations, components, and patterns over and over again allows them to focus on more important things, like creating or iterating on features, flows, and user experiences.

Freeing designers from re-creating the same design elements over and over again allows them to focus on more important things, like iteration, new features, and user experience.

Tools for the job

I stated at the start of this book that it would be futile to dive too much into the technology side of design systems in print. Design tools evolve so fast that the words I freeze in time in this book may no longer apply by the time you read this. With that said, I don't want to leave you empty-handed, so I'll talk a little about design tools to consider.

Where Photoshop was once the industry standard for web designers, the need for a vector based, dynamic, and specialist user interface design tool became clear circa 2015(-ish). There are now a host of options out there! Below is a brief introduction to just a few of them, and there are more up-to-date resources and links on this book's website **(8.2)**.

In the beginning of this revolution of new design tools, Sketch **(8.3)** quickly rose to fame as the popular choice for web and product designers. Sketch's text styles and responsive, nested symbols (for editable, reusable components) — paired with Sketch Library **(8.4)** — are superb for working with and managing a design library. This is the design toolset I've used since 2016 for web design and to create design systems that power large design teams and entire suites of products, so I can speak first-hand to its excellent performance.

I've also created a Skillshare class **(8.5)** showing how I currently (at the time of this book's publication) set up symbols in a design library in Sketch.

While I have no experience using the following design tools, I've heard good things:

- Framer X **(8.6)** is a design tool doing amazing things to bridge the gap between design and code. You can create interactive, animated, reusable components. You can even design with React components from production (i.e. your real product).
- Adobe XD **(8.7)** is a design tool to keep an eye on. It's been in a work in progress for sometime now, but they have a great team working on it and its progression is encouraging.
- For something different, Figma **(8.8)** is a browser-based design tool (not software) that allows multiple designers (and other stakeholders) to work simultaneously on a design.

And then there are designers who consider any **code editor** to be a design tool — using production code, 'sandbox' test environments, designing in the browser, and prototyping with 'real' (built) components. I count myself among those designers — I love to iterate on responsive designs and animations live in the browser, to really hone the design and user experience.

At the end of the day, I'm not here to tell you what tools to use. **They're just tools.** It's up to you to discover which processes and tools work best for your team's preferences, comfort, skill sets, and aptitudes. And it's probably a good idea to agree on one tool, which your whole team uses — so you avoid different versions of the same design system elements being created and used in different software!

Naming conventions

As I've mentioned before, naming conventions are important in design systems. Each text style, colour, component, and pattern in your design system should have a unique name, and it's important that the name you use in your design library, matches the code and the documentation.

The idea is this: if you state the name of a text style, colour, component, or pattern in a design mockup — or in a product discussion — then the other people on your team (designers, developers, and product managers) should either know exactly what you're referring to, or be able to look it up in your documentation (aka the source of truth).

It helps to be systematic about your naming conventions. It seems boring, but for example, naming text styles "Title 1" through "Title 5" (reducing in size the larger the number) is a lot easier to understand than naming them something like "Daisy" or "Yosemite". While it might be fun to come up with humorous or descriptive names for system elements — your naming conventions need to make sense to more people than just you and your friends on your team. They need to resonate with the whole team, new people onboarding to the team, and semantically make sense in the code.

8.3 sketch.com

8.4 sketch.com/docs/libraries/

8.5 skl.sh/2xWBObZ

8.6 framer.com

8.7 adobe.com/products/xd.html

8.8 figma.com

Title 1

erik abel

Title 2

Showcasing surf culture, art and photography

Title 3

Showcasing surf culture, art and photography

Title 4

Showcasing surf culture, art and photography

Copy 1

Showcasing surf culture, art and photography.

Copy 2

Showcasing surf culture, art and photography.

FIG 8.1 Text styles with semantic names from clubofthewaves.com

The example (FIG 8.1) from the Club of the Waves website demonstrates simple and semantic naming conventions for foundational text styles.

It also helps if your naming conventions are scalable. As digital products evolve, new scenarios call for new foundational elements (like colours and text styles), or new components and patterns. If you have a colour named "Ocean Blue", what happens when you need to add a second blue, or a lighter shade of the same blue? Do you then have "Ocean Blue", "Lighter Ocean Blue", "Winter Blue", "Sky Blue", and so on? You need a more semantic (i.e. logical) approach to naming.

For example, following a colour audit of their website, Hipmunk (8.9) discovered they were not only using a wide array of colours for warnings and errors, but the names they had given these colours were likely contributing to so many new colours being introduced. Below (FIG 8.2) is a sample of what their audit discovered:

Faded Red   Warning Pink   Hip Error   Alert Red   Warning Red   Red

FIG 8.2 A colour audit reveals none semantic names and rogue colours

A name like "Alert Red" works on its own — it's clear to designers and developers what the colour's intent is. However, if you also have "Warning Red", "Warning Pink", and "Hip Error" — like Hipmunk do — then you have a problem.

Later in this chapter, we'll look at how to create and name a system of colours using a similar approach to Google Material (8.10), who created a range of

8.9 uxdesign.cc/hipmunk-design-system-part-1-colors-ux-case-study-1ac99806aabd

8.10 material.io/design/color/the-color-system.html

colours based off one brand colour. Something like this **(FIG 8.3)**:

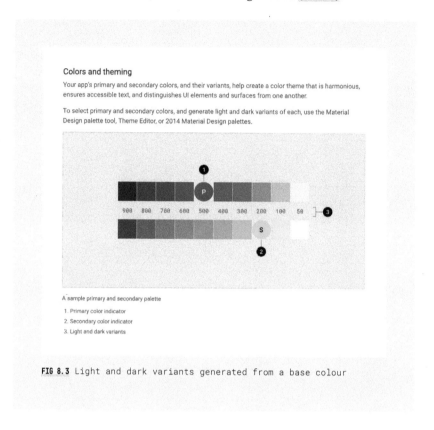

Colors and theming

Your app's primary and secondary colors, and their variants, help create a color theme that is harmonious, ensures accessible text, and distinguishes UI elements and surfaces from one another.

To select primary and secondary colors, and generate light and dark variants of each, use the Material Design palette tool, Theme Editor, or 2014 Material Design palettes.

A sample primary and secondary palette

1. Primary color indicator
2. Secondary color indicator
3. Light and dark variants

FIG 8.3 Light and dark variants generated from a base colour

Note their numeric naming conventions. The higher the number, the darker the colour.

> "The Material Design color system uses an organized approach to applying color to your UI. Dark and light variants of each color can then be applied to your UI in different ways. The variants help create a color theme that is harmonious, ensuring accessible text, and distinguishing UI elements and surfaces from one another."

8.11 brand.opentable.com/color/

You don't have to assign numeric values to make naming conventions work, but you do need some logic in place. In stark contrast to Google Material, OpenTable **(8.11)** name their two primary brand colours "Early Girl" and "Blueberry" **(FIG 8.4)**:

FIG 8.4 OpenTable's colour system documentation

On their own they are arguably confusing, but they make more sense when you see them in the context of their secondary brand colours **(FIG 8.5)**. Their primary brand colour, "Blueberry" is blue, but they also have two colours named "Blue" and "Teal" in their secondary palette.

You can certainly argue OpenTable are walking a fine line, semantically, but in this case, their use of a 'human' name for their brand primary colours is fitting to their brand ethos. It would get messy if they named all their colours so randomly, but confining the quirky names to the primary brand colours, then using more distinctive naming conventions for their other colours, creates just enough distinction for it to work.

We'll cover the logic behind OpenTable's use of colour more in the next chapter.

FIG 8.5 Primary and secondary colour palettes and their use cases

Colour system

Colour is tricky. It's easy to say: "Our brand colours are X, Y, and Z. Only use these colours." But then, with such a limited colour palette, what do you use for a hover state? What do you use to communicate an error? If you want to create a subtle differential in content using a background colour, what do you use?

A colour audit I conducted at a previous job uncovered several different shades of the 'same' colour. The actual brand colour had been lost over time.

We've all done it. You 'need' a new colour. You open up your colour picker and drag the picker slightly up/down/left/right, picking the colour that feels right. This is 'fine' for one-off website projects, but not for a team of designers working on the same product(s). If other designers on your team do the same — picking random colours, multiple times, in different scenarios — over time, this results in numerous hex values (e.g. #b85c35) in your CSS, used erratically and inconsistently throughout your product. Not very systematic, is it?

I advise you to look at colours as a system within a system. Think about these things, relating to colour:

• Your brand identity: the core colours of your brand.
• Headers and copy: typically dark text on a light background.

- Scenarios like navigation, links, errors, and success states.
- Backgrounds and subtle deviations in background colours.

To combat designers picking random colours, I advise your design system include a range of colours to cover these brand and digital content scenarios. This is where Sass — which we discussed briefly in the "Code Audits" section of "An Iterative Approach" chapter — can be a game-changer. For the non-developers: think of Sass as an advanced form of CSS. It allows us to — among other things — systematically create new colours. We can take a base colour and darken it by 10%, lighten it by 10%, or adjust it by any percentage we like.

P.S. Don't worry if you don't know Sass. Work with a developer. It won't be hard for a front-end developer to spin this up for you. You can also use an online Sass colour generator (8.12) to get the color values you need. And if you want to learn Sass, I recommend the book, *Sass for Web Designers* (8.13) by Dan Cederholm (8.14). This is the book I bought and worked through when I first learned Sass.

Decide on a base colour for each (brand) colour in your system. For example, your base colour for blue could be: #62a5d7. From that base colour, use Sass to create a range of colours based on that value, like so (FIG 8.6):

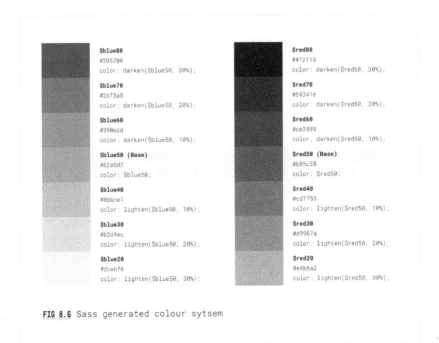

$blue80
#205780
color: darken($blue50, 30%);

$blue70
#2b73a8
color: darken($blue50, 20%);

$blue60
#398ecd
color: darken($blue50, 10%);

$blue50 (Base)
#62a5d7
color: $blue50;

$blue40
#8bbce1
color: lighten($blue50, 10%);

$blue30
#b3d4ec
color: lighten($blue50, 20%);

$blue20
#dcebf6
color: lighten($blue50, 30%);

$red80
#412113
color: darken($red50, 30%);

$red70
#69341e
color: darken($red50, 20%);

$red60
#ce3939
color: darken($red50, 10%);

$red50 (Base)
#b85c35
color: $red50;

$red40
#cd7753
color: lighten($red50, 10%);

$red30
#d9967a
color: lighten($red50, 20%);

$red20
#e4b6a2
color: lighten($red50, 30%);

FIG 8.6 Sass generated colour sytsem

In the example **(FIG 8.6)**, note the two base colours in the middle of both ranges: "$blue50" and "$red50". For each base colour I've created three darker variants by darkening the colour in 10% increments, and three lighter variants by lightening the colour in 10% increments.

A colour system like this makes it easy to choose colours for different scenarios without the need to introduce new, rogue colours and code. For example, from our colour system pictured above, you might choose $red50 as the background colour for a button, and choose $red60 as the hover state, like in the following example **(FIG 8.7)**.

The great thing about this Sass colour system is its scalability. This process can be applied to any brand colour, creating a versatile range of colours with minimal effort. Best of all: if you change a brand colour, you need only change the one base colour and all other colours in that range will update automatically in your Sass!

FIG 8.7 Colour system at work with different button states

Naming colours

As we discussed at the beginning of this chapter, the naming conventions you use for colours should be the same in the design and code. If a designer says to use the "red30" colour, then the developer should know what they mean and easily be able to apply that colour.

It might seem extreme, but to avoid any conflict in this area, I like to name colours (exactly) the same as they appear in the code, as Sass variables. Anything you can do to bridge the gap between design and engineering is a positive.

Let's break this naming convention down:

Firstly: in the code, Sass variables are preceded by a "$".

Secondly: assigning a numeric value to each colour in your range — from light to dark — avoids any confusion around vague terminology like "darker" or "lighter". I advise starting at something like 50 (or 100), to avoid negative numbers. In our example:

- "50" is always the base colour.
- "60" is darker, "70" is darker still, then "80".
- "40" is lighter, "30" is lighter still, then "20".

I use two digits, as opposed to one (e.g. 50 instead of 5), so you have the flexibility to add as great a range of colours as you need. For example, you could later decide to go in 5% increments — instead of 10% — like in the following example (FIG 8.8), adding a $blue55 between the $blue50 and $blue60 colours.

I would recommend not having too great a range (of colour variants) in your colour system. Remember the constraints we talked about earlier — constraints can be a good thing.

Try it for yourself

You can access and edit the Sass colour system used in our example on CodePen (8.15). Access the CodePen link, then go ahead and change the hex value (e.g. #62a5d7) of one of the three Sass variables (e.g. $blue50) and see what happens. You can also use this code to create your own colour system!

Guidelines for colour

Another good point to consider when defining a colour palette for your brand are the use cases and intent of each colour. Rather than having a mass palette of colours that can be used in any number of ways, it's smart to define colour groups, like for example, 'Primary', 'Secondary', 'Utility', 'Accent', 'Tertiary', and so on. Let's unpack what I mean by this.

8.12 scg.ar-ch.org

8.13 abookapart.com/products/sass-for-web-designers

8.14 simplebits.com

8.15 codepen.io/roomfive/pen/ybYQZP

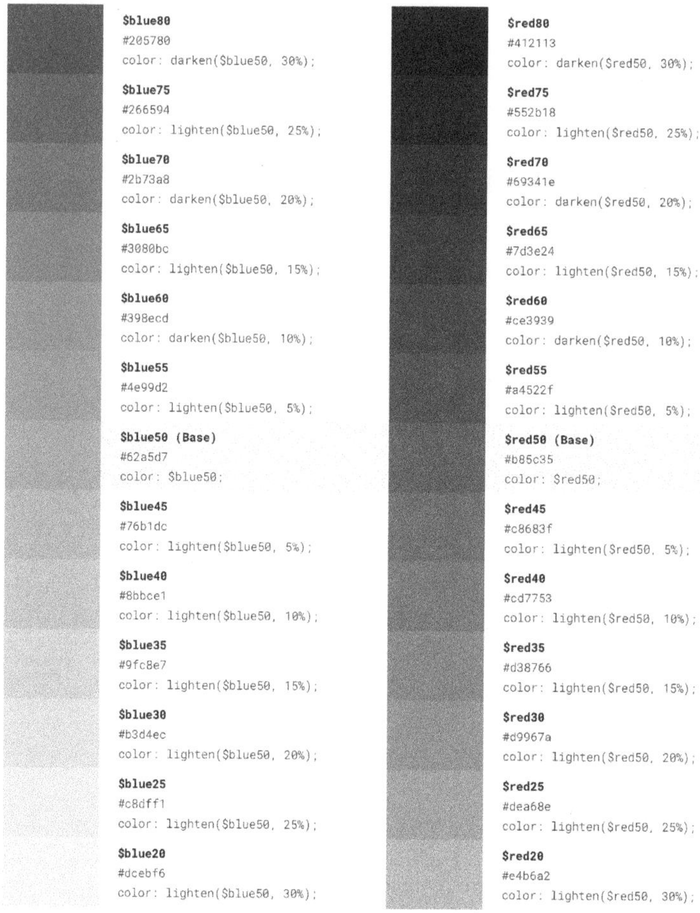

$blue80
#205780
color: darken($blue50, 30%);

$blue75
#266594
color: lighten($blue50, 25%);

$blue70
#2b73a8
color: darken($blue50, 20%);

$blue65
#3080bc
color: lighten($blue50, 15%);

$blue60
#398ecd
color: darken($blue50, 10%);

$blue55
#4e99d2
color: lighten($blue50, 5%);

$blue50 (Base)
#62a5d7
color: $blue50;

$blue45
#76b1dc
color: lighten($blue50, 5%);

$blue40
#8bbce1
color: lighten($blue50, 10%);

$blue35
#9fc8e7
color: lighten($blue50, 15%);

$blue30
#b3d4ec
color: lighten($blue50, 20%);

$blue25
#c8dff1
color: lighten($blue50, 25%);

$blue20
#dcebf6
color: lighten($blue50, 30%);

$red80
#412113
color: darken($red50, 30%);

$red75
#552b18
color: lighten($red50, 25%);

$red70
#69341e
color: darken($red50, 20%);

$red65
#7d3e24
color: lighten($red50, 15%);

$red60
#ce3939
color: darken($red50, 10%);

$red55
#a4522f
color: lighten($red50, 5%);

$red50 (Base)
#b85c35
color: $red50;

$red45
#c8683f
color: lighten($red50, 5%);

$red40
#cd7753
color: lighten($red50, 10%);

$red35
#d38766
color: lighten($red50, 15%);

$red30
#d9967a
color: lighten($red50, 20%);

$red25
#dea68e
color: lighten($red50, 25%);

$red20
#e4b6a2
color: lighten($red50, 30%);

FIG 8.8 Sass generated colour sytsem

Primary brand colours

Primary brand colours are arguably the most important. They are typically
the core colours that make up your brand. For example, EE's primary brand
colours are aqua and yellow, where Coca-Cola's are red and white **(FIG 8.9)**.
Primary brand colours tend to be used for prominent elements like calls to
action and backgrounds. They may also be used for large headers, but are
less likely to be used for copy (if only for their accessibility). For example the

yellow in EE's brand (**FIG 8.9**), used for copy text, wouldn't be legible on a white background.

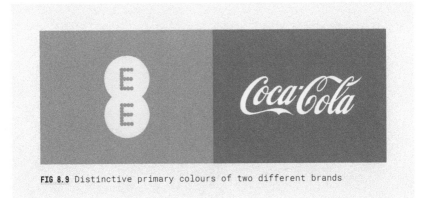

FIG 8.9 Distinctive primary colours of two different brands

Utility colours

Utility colours tend to be colours like black and shades of gray. They are used for copy and headers. They pair well and contrast with the primary colours, to create distinction and hierarchy. Keep accessibility in mind when defining utility colours, making sure any grayscale colours you use for copy are legible on a light background colour.

Secondary, tertiary, or accent colours

Any other colours in your palette — in addition to primary and utility — are more of a 'supporting cast'. Secondary, tertiary, accent — or whatever you call them — colours should be used less frequently than your core primary and utility colours. These colours can be functional, like red for warnings or green for success. Or they can be complementary, giving you greater flexibility in your designs for things like background colours, for example.

Limited text styles

Moving on from colour. You should explore a wide variety of scenarios to discover the different text styles needed in your product. Aim to consistently use a limited number of text styles, and only create new text styles when you need them. You probably don't need that many.

I would aim for only a few header styles, and a few copy styles.

Depending on your brand and use cases of your design system, you may want to keep the application of these text styles flexible, or document specific use cases for each style. For example, a specific header style might be so large and imposing that the documentation instructs limited and specific use cases for it. Take the example below, from the Plasma design system **(8.16)**. This

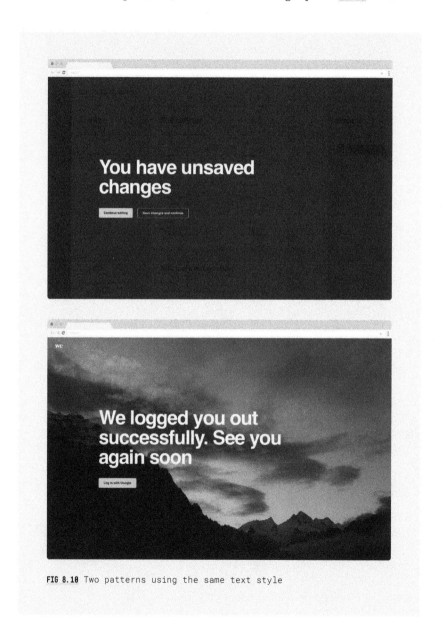

FIG 8.10 Two patterns using the same text style

particular text style is so large, it's only intended (and documented) use cases are in the two patterns **(FIG 8.10)**:

Similarly, a larger copy style might be intended only for opening paragraphs of copy or used to distinguish quotes. You might have a text style intended to be the default text style for all body copy in articles, blog posts, web pages, and so on. And a particularly small copy style might be limited to use cases like captions, footnotes, and warnings.

Importantly, you should document any formatting guidelines for each text style. If your team doesn't understand the significance of, or logic behind each text style, then how do you expect them to apply them correctly?

Title 1

erik abel

Title 2

Surf art by Erik Abel

Title 3

A look behind the scenes

FIG 8.11 Text styles from clubofthewaves.com

8.16 roomfive.net/plasma-design-system/

Take the example (FIG 8.11). Looking only at three text styles from this design system, the following guidelines apply:

- Headers should never end with a period ("."}.
- All header styles except 'Title 1' should be sentence case (with the exception of names of places and people).
- 'Title 1' should always be lowercase.

Editable components

Establishing a shared library of editable components is key to unlocking the speed, ease, and efficiency design systems can bring to the design process. I'm talking about designers being able to:

1. Easily and quickly insert pre-made components into their designs.
2. Edit the component's content.
3. Switch between its different states (we'll cover those next).
4. Sync any updates made to the component (we'll cover this in the "Maintaining a Design System" chapter).

Perhaps most importantly, a library of editable components practically removes any chance of designers deviating from the established system components, as you can control what is and isn't editable about each component. So for a button: you want designers on your team to be able to edit the text on the button, but you don't want them to edit the font family, font weight, font size, font colour, background colour, border-radius, height, and so on.

It's important to lock down the design of components in a shared library, however, if you do want to edit one instance of a component, some design tools make it easy to do so. For example, Sketch symbols (8.17) allow you to set overrides for specific parts of a component (e.g. you can edit just the text, or the icon and the text).

Continuing with our Sketch symbols example: as well as being editable, symbols are also responsive, and are intended to be reused multiple times in your design mockups. The idea is that you edit the master symbol in one place, and your change is applied in every instance the symbol is used! This can be really powerful in designs where a component is used dozens of times in different mockups, artboards, and scenarios.

The following screenshot (FIG 8.12) shows a symbol with the Overrides panel open to the right of the screen. The example shows that I can only edit the text ("View photographer") and nothing else about this particular button component.

FIG 8.12 Editable symbol with overrides in Sketch

I would love to show you how powerful a design library of system components can be, but it's hard to do so in print. So I've created a Skillshare class **(8.18)** showing how I currently (at the time of this book's publication) set up editable, responsive, and syncable symbols in Sketch.

FIG 8.13 Colour system at work with different button states

Cover all states of components

Your design system and library should include all possible states for each component. For example, a button might have a normal, hover, and disabled state. The image above **(FIG 8.13)** shows three states for the same button component — its normal, hover, and disabled states.

Aside from *obvious* states like a button's hover state, or a text input's placeholder and value states — remember that all or most of your system components will likely have different states to cover a wide variety of product interactions and scenarios. For example, components like radio buttons and checkboxes come in 'checked' and 'unchecked' states. They can also be grouped by 'fieldset', requiring a 'legend' to make sense of what the options are (for accessibility and a good user experience).

Below **(FIG 8.14)** is an example of design system documentation for radio buttons, with a visual demonstrating the different states, and text explaining the what, why, where, and when of using this component. The components seen in this visual **(FIG 8.14)** are all easily accessible by the team working with this design system — which the Skillshare class **(8.18)** mentioned earlier covers how to create and setup.

FIG 8.14 plasma.guide/form-specs/

Providing your designers with easy access to these different states, types, and groupings of components (plus documentation) is a real timesaver, and ensures consistent systematic design. It also removes the guesswork for developers; if you fail to define the styles for these alternate states, they may go

8.17 sketch.com/docs/symbols/

8.18 skl.sh/2xWBObZ

rogue and invent their own, sometimes with less than desirable results.

Pattern library

Creating a library of established patterns can be as valuable as a component library. For example, if you're creating a new template (or page) for a website, chances are that web page will use the same global footer (pattern) as the rest of your website. Creating an easily accessible (and insertable) footer pattern will save your design team a lot of time, and avoid any confusion on the development side.

The image below **(FIG 8.15)** is an example of a responsive footer pattern — ready and easily accessible to drop into any design mockups.

FIG 8.15 A responsive pattern ready to insert into design mockups

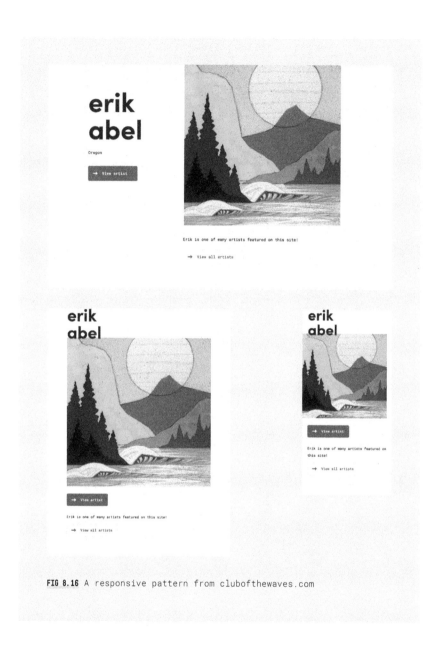

FIG 8.16 A responsive pattern from clubofthewaves.com

Responsive design

I've always tried to encourage responsive design with visual design teams I've worked with. Your design library can help with this. At the time of writing this, design tools like Sketch are brilliant for creating responsive components, but not so great for (some) responsive patterns. Patterns are more susceptible to things like content wrapping, variable heights, and stacking of content (e.g. 3 columns on desktop become 1 column on mobile).

If the design tool you use can't effectively achieve a responsive pattern, then your design library should at least cover how the pattern appears at different browser widths or device sizes. For example, see how the footer pattern (FIG 8.15) and the following example pattern (FIG 8.16) respond at three different browser widths.

Having responsive, established design system patterns like the example above, designed and ready to easily drop into future design mockups is a valuable timesaver, and ensures your design team don't recreate them — slightly different each time — introducing unintentional amendments to the code, or rogue elements being introduced.

Design tokens and Sass variables

This is one of the rare points in this book where we'll cover a more code-focussed topic. While the execution of design tokens and Sass variables is a task for a developer, and very much a code-based thing, they are based on systematic design decisions (made by designers). So let's cover it — that way you can sound super smart when you ask developers about it! ;)

As this is a project that requires designers and developers working together, my advice is to strike up a conversation with the developer(s) on your team that cares most about the front-end, and ask them about creating Sass variables and design tokens.

We talked about Sass variables relating to colour earlier in this chapter. Sass variables are a valuable asset in design systems. They are snippets of code used repeatedly throughout a code base, but controlled from one central source. If you change a Sass variable or design token at the source, it will change everywhere it is used!

In the words of Salesforce's Lightning design system:

> *"Design tokens are the visual design atoms of the design system — specifically, they are named entities that store visual design attributes. We use them in place of hard-coded values (such as hex values for color or pixel values for spacing) in order to maintain a scalable and consistent visual system for UI development."*

The Lightning design system's documentation has an entire page dedicated to its design tokens, categorised by their function. The screenshot **(FIG 8.17)** shows their design tokens relating to colour.

Design tokens are very similar to Sass variables, in that they are (ultimately) snippets of code used repeatedly throughout a product, controlled from one central source. Sass variables and design tokens can work harmoniously together to give you a great deal of control over the system at large.

FIG 8.17 lightningdesignsystem.com/design-tokens/

Strike up a conversation with the developer on your team that cares most about the front-end, and ask them about creating Sass variables and design tokens.

The difference between a Sass variable and a design token

A Sass variable is a generic, reusable value — it can be applied in a great number of different scenarios. For example, it could be a brand colour, which can be applied to anything from headers to copy, backgrounds, links, buttons, icons, and so on.

A design token is a more specific value, but it's also reusable. A design token can serve specific purposes, like specifying:

- Section colours
- Background colours for use in specific scenarios or patterns
- Small spacing, versus large spacing
- Font sizes
- 5% opacity, versus 50% opacity
- Global states for 'disabled' and 'active'

Design tokens essentially store design decisions — like colour, size, and space — which can be systematically applied throughout a product.

Use cases

If you only introduce Sass variables in your CSS, you'll have made a big improvement. But even Sass variables have their drawbacks, systematically speaking. For example, take these two scenarios: **Option 1** and **Option 2**. In both cases we want to apply a background colour to a website (applying CSS to the body tag).

```
Design token

$color-background-light: #ffffff;


The design token can be applied in the CSS like so:

body {
  background-color: $color-background-light;
}

FIG 8.18 Option 1: design token
```

Option 1 (design token)

The first option uses a design token. We'll use a real design token from the Lightning design system, called: `$color-background-light`. This design token is simply the colour white (#ffffff). Our design token and CSS look like this (**FIG 8.18**).

Option 2 (Sass variable)

The second option instead uses a Sass variable to apply the background colour. Our Sass variable and CSS look like the following (**FIG 8.19**):

```
Sass variable:

$white: #ffffff;


The Sass variable can be applied in the CSS like so:

body {
  background-color: $white;
}
```

FIG 8.19 Option 2: Sass variable

So far so good. Both options look very similar, and both work fine!

Now, consider this:

- The Sass variable we used ($white) is incredibly **generic**, and is used in dozens of places throughout our website. It could be used for text colours, svg colours, or any other object that is white.
- In contrast, the design token we used ($color-background-light) is **specifically** used as a background colour.

Scenario: we want to change our website's background colour to be a slightly off-white colour (or any light colour).

1. In Option 1 (design token) we'd be okay, as we'd be making a global change to a design token intended only for scenarios just like or similar to this one. Changing from white to a new colour will likely be fine.

2. In Option 2 (Sass variable) we have a problem. Our Sass variable is used in several places — changing the colour of the Sass variable to a new colour could cause problems elsewhere in our website.

It's complicated, I know. But you should consider these caveats when deciding on design tokens and their use cases in your system.

BuzzFeed's Solid design system uses design tokens for specific use cases of

Text Colors

Solid provides a range of text colors, as well as some lighter and darker variations. When selecting a color for a block of text, it's important to take into account the documented usages below (using green text only for success messaging, for instance).

.text-gray #222222, $text-gray

This is the darkest gray and default text color.

.text-gray-lighter #666666, $text-gray-lighter

This is a little lighter gray.

.text-gray-lightest #999999, $text-gray-lightest

The lightest of all the grays.

.text-red #ee3322, $text-red

This is red text for both brand text/headlines and error messaging. Be careful when mixing!

.text-pink #f43192, $text-pink

This is pink text.

.text-orange #f47f16, $text-orange

This is orange text for warning messaging.

.text-promoted-orange #f7ad19, $text-promoted-orange

This is orange text for ad unit disclosures. Don't use for anything else!

.text-blue #0f65ef, $text-blue

This is our standard link color. It's on links by default.

.text-purple #6645dd, $text-purple

This is purple text.

.text-green #68af15, $text-green

This is green text for success messaging.

.text-white #ffffff, $text-white

White text for dark backgrounds.

FIG 8.20 solid.buzzfeed.com/colors.html

colour in text **(FIG 8.20)**, links, and even SVG fill colours.

Notice: Solid's design token $text-green is intended to be used to make text green (obviously), but it's not saying specifically what green colour. Designating a token for a specific scenario is good, since you may use a darker shade of green for text (for legibility purposes), and a lighter shade of green for icons or background colours — in which case you could also have tokens like: $icon-green and $background-green.

Lonely Planet's design system, Rizzo **(FIG 8.21)**, includes design token documentation for colour that are clearly and effectively presented and organised by function (e.g. "UI background and borders", or "section colours"). A really neat feature on this page is the ability to copy the hex value to your clipboard simply by clicking on the colour.

FIG 8.21 rizzo.lonelyplanet.com/styleguide/design-elements/ui-colours

Combining Sass variables and design tokens, for the win

If you want to get really smart, you can combine the two together to form the most efficient, scalable, and easily updatable system **(FIG 8.23)**:

```
Design token and Sass variable combined:

$white: #ffffff;
$color-background-light: $white;


Our Option 1 and 2 scenario (from earlier) is now a little
easier to solve:

$white: #ffffff;
$off-white: #f9f9f9;
$color-background-light: $white;
$color-background-light: $off-white;
```

FIG 8.23 Combining Sass variables with design tokens

172

Now for a full example! Don't worry if you don't know code, I've attempted to break down what's happening to show Sass variables, design tokens, CSS, and HTML at work **(FIG 8.24)**:

```
Sass variable:
$blue50: #62A5D7;


Design token, using the Sass variable:
$brand-color-primary: $blue50;


Design token applied to a text style in the CSS:
.primary-header {
  color: $brand-color-primary;
}


CSS applied to a header in the HTML:
<h1 class="primary-header">Hello</h1>
```

FIG 8.24 Sass variables, design tokens, CSS, and HTML

The above code gives us this in the browser:

Now, to use our same example again. If we add a new Sass variable ($red50), then change our $brand-primary design token to use $red50 instead of $blue50, the change will 'auto-magically' take effect in the front-end (website). Like so **(FIG 8.25)**:

```
Sass variable:

$blue50: #62A5D7;
$red50: #b85c35;


Design token, using the Sass variable:

$brand-color-primary: $blue50;
$brand-color-primary: $red50;
```

FIG 8.25 Combining Sass variables with design tokens

The above code gives us this in the browser:

This might seem like a simple change (in our example), but imagine these design tokens used in dozens or hundreds of places throughout a product! You can see how powerful design tokens can be.

Not just for colour!

We've only looked at colour so far, but Sass variables and design tokens can be used for anything from font families to font sizes, line heights, spacing (margins and padding), radius, shadow, and so on. They can be used for anything that's reused consistently throughout a product. For example, the Vue design system documentation **(FIG 8.22)** also includes design tokens for spacing.

It's good practice to use consistent spacing in digital design, and chances are you've defined some logic for that spacing. If you're obsessive like me, you might like working with simple numbers that are divisible by 5 — something like: 5px, 10px, 15px, 20px, 30px, 60px, 90px, 120px. Or if you're using a grid system — like the '8-point grid system' — you would use: 8px, 16px, 24px, 32px, 40px, 48px, 56px, and so on.

FIG 8.26 `primer.style/css/support/spacing`

GitHub's Primer design system uses the 8-point grid system, and they've included a page **(FIG 8.26)** in their documentation relating to their variables used for consistent spacing. Notice in their system: it's smart that they've additionally added a variable for 4px. A minimum spacing of 8px is a little limiting.

Designer access to code

I'd like to make an argument for granting designers (not just developers) access to the code. This will scare some, and excite others. Developers can be very protective of their code bases, with good reason. However, they also don't love getting 'bugged' by designers to make (seemingly) small updates to the code. The easiest way to avoid this is for designers to gain access to the code themselves. Design tokens make this process so much easier.

Even if a designer only has access to the design tokens and Sass variables, they can achieve a lot — quickly — without disturbing developers. If they want to change the colour blue used in X scenarios, they can. If they want to increase the space between X and Y elements throughout the product, they can.

Designers that code

Web designers having even a little knowledge of code will go a long way. I can't recommend enough that designers get comfortable with — at least — CSS and HTML. It simply will make you a better web designer if you gain a deeper understanding of your craft. You may be surprised by how much you enjoy it. It's fun and very satisfying to bring your own creations to life, and iterate on them in the browser!

That said, even if you're not planning to build websites yourself, a little knowledge of code is all you need to update things like design tokens. I really believe that anything that brings designers and developers closer together is a good thing. Speak to the developers on your team about gaining access to the code.

If you want to go deeper into the realms of 'the role of development in design', check out this article (8.19) I wrote on responsive design.

Tracking and organising system tasks

As you may be realising, creating a design library is a lot of work! You're going to need to get organised, keep track of 'to-dos', and know who's doing what (on your team and/or across your different teams). Everyone has their preferences for tracking tasks and delegating. Some use tools like GitHub Issues, Basecamp, Dropbox Paper, Asana, or Jira. My tool of choice for tracking massive projects like product and system design is Trello (8.20).

I love the simplicity of Trello. It allows you to create boards to track projects, milestones, or sprints. Within each board, you can create cards to represent tasks. Within each card, you can describe the task, and create checklists

8.19 medium.com/@andrewcouldwell/responsive-design-af7a1f14b991

8.20 trello.com

8.21 roomfive.net/adobe-portfolio/

for everything that needs to happen to complete the task. You can sort the checklists by sub-headers, drag and drop everything to re-order and prioritise, set a due date, add attachments, assign cards to different team members, and your team can comment on tasks.

The example screenshot **(FIG 8.27)** is of my Trello board from 2015/16, which I used while designing Adobe Portfolio **(8.21)**:

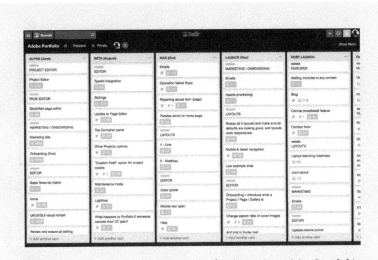

FIG 8.27 My Trello borad from 2015 while designing Adobe Portfolio

The columns **(FIG 8.27)** are different boards I created to mark milestones and track tasks (cards) that needed to be completed. For context, all the green markers signify that I'd completed those tasks (bearing in mind this is an old Trello board!) — back in 2015/16, there would have been a sea of red markers on this board, which I gradually turned to green over time!

This was a massive project spanning system design, product design, web design, marketing, and brand. Organisation for so many tasks and deadlines was crucial. This was my first real test of Trello, and it served me well! The text is small, but perhaps you can make out **(FIG 8.27)** that some of the tasks only had one checklist item to complete the task, where others had 20+ checklist items.

One of my favourite features is when you 'tick' tasks off a checklist — or add more tasks — a percentage complete bar dynamically fills to show your progress. It's painfully nerdy, I know, but there's something very satisfying about checking tasks off and seeing your progress. You can see in the screenshot below (**FIG 8.28**) that the first checklist is 100% complete, but the second checklist is only 82% complete.

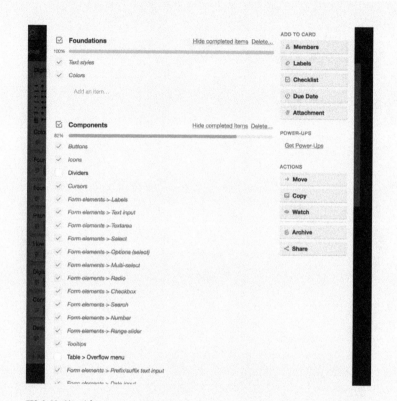

FIG 8.28 Checklists to track to-dos and progress of tasks

Look how far we've come!

We've covered a lot in this chapter, from creating a shared design system library of editable components, to pattern libraries, responsive design, naming conventions, working with colours, text styles, spacing, designers writing code, and creating design tokens. My hope is that you now have a good idea of how to go about systematising your designs and working more efficiently as a team.

Next we're going to talk about a very important part of creating a design system: the documentation.

DOC—UMENT EVERY—THING!

09

Documentation is fundamentally important for design systems. Don't be fooled by this chapter appearing so late in this book — this isn't an indication that you should leave documentation until last. You shouldn't. You should document design and code as you progress, as part of your process.

More than a style guide

A system wouldn't be a system without rules and guidelines, which is why documentation is one of the main things that distinguishes a design system from a simple style guide or a UI kit.

A 'UI kit' needs less introduction than a style guide — you've probably seen UI kits on Dribbble and Behance, or as free downloads promoting a service or vendor. They look cool, but that's all they are: just a random assortment of *cool-looking* design elements. They often deal with ideals, and can be put to use any way you wish — because they didn't (really) have a specific use case in the first place, as they're often not based in reality, with real content, problems, users, or businesses.

Where a UI kit could be applied to anything, a style guide is usually more comprehensive and focussed on a real product. 'Style guide' might be one of the most confusing terms in digital design. You might even disagree with my definition of it, but as we've covered in this book: speaking the same language, or at least having a shared understanding is important. So, let's define what style guides are...

Style guides are a valuable addition to web design projects; they're something I almost always deliver to a client alongside responsive web page designs. They single out foundations (e.g. text styles and colours) and components (e.g. buttons and inputs) from a design — identifying them as deliberate design decisions that are used consistently throughout a product. A style guide also covers things that aren't obvious in design mockups — things like hover states, error states, and so on.

A style guide is a form of documentation, but not necessarily a design system (in its simplest of forms). They are valuable for developers to build from, and they keep designers in-check, but they lack *depth*. They showcase design system elements, but they generally don't explain *why*, *where*, *when*, and *how* to use any of those elements.

A simple style guide is like a diagram of all the elements that make up a piece of IKEA furniture without the instructions telling you how to assemble them. You might build something that resembles the picture on the box, or you might create something entirely different.

The Disqus style guide (**FIG 9.1**) is a good example of a simple style guide, which documents the basics like colour, typography, and brand, but doesn't go into detail of how to use them. This can be useful, and it serves a purpose, but it leaves a lot to interpretation.

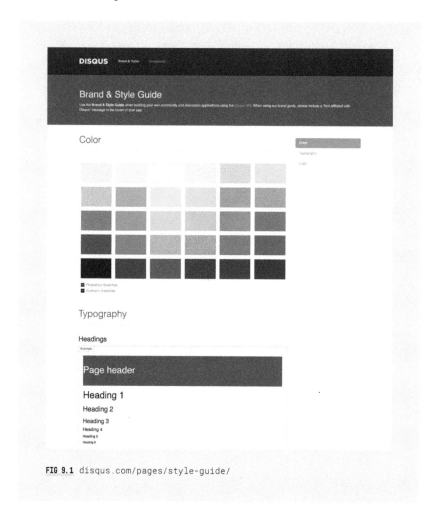

FIG 9.1 disqus.com/pages/style-guide/

All this isn't to say that if you don't have documentation, you don't have a design system. That's not true, so long as you've been designing systematically. It's more to say that if you're going to all the effort of designing and building a design system, then you should do everything possible to ensure people use it 'properly' and sustainably.

The basics

Documentation acts as a source of truth — a reference point. If you're unsure how to approach, do, write, format, design, or build something, the documentation is where you'll find the answer! It benefits everyone, from the most junior to the most senior members of your team, and it's great for onboarding new team members.

Documentation:

- Demystifies our design and code decisions.
- Helps to keep all people working with the system on the same page.
- Helps to onboard new team members.
- Tracks revisions to the system, to keep everyone in the loop.
- ~~It makes your company look really smart!~~ Helps recruit new talent.

Better together

As I've emphasised throughout this book, when creating a design system it's important to be mindful that you won't be the only person who works with it. We make very deliberate design decisions when we design systematically, meaning the decisions we make about font size, text styles, spacing, colour, and animation are made for a reason. These decisions are then applied repetitively and consistently across multiple elements in the system.

The guidelines and decisions you make when designing a system are no good just in your head. They shouldn't be communicated on a 'need to know' basis. Everybody needs to know.

The key is to **make documentation part of your (design and build) process**. Don't leave documentation until the end, or as an afterthought. If you do, it might never get done, or you'll forget what you're actually documenting.

Don't get caught up in how your documentation looks. Just get the reasoning behind your design decisions out of your head and into some form of documentation. You can *make it look pretty later*. We'll talk more about how to format and present the documentation later in this chapter. First, a few further points to demonstrate why documenting design systems is important.

A simple style guide is like a diagram of all the elements that make up a piece of IKEA furniture without the instructions telling you how to assemble them.

You might build something that resembles the picture on the box, or you might create something entirely different. This is why you need documentation.

Don't leave documentation until last

Documentation should never be left to the end of a project. Don't just take it from me — Airbnb **(9.1)** regretted not documenting sooner:

> *"...This project required us to operate within a tight timeline, which caused us to overlook some of the documentation process. Lacking thorough documentation created some confusion that could have been avoided. Just like with coding, documenting systems as they are created is paramount to the process. It has to be done sooner or later, and documenting throughout the creation process allows for smoother decision-making."*

To put some of what we've covered thus far in this chapter into perspective, I'll reflect on my experience back in 2014-16 when I was designing the Adobe Portfolio product **(9.2)** at Behance. I'll be honest, I didn't progress the design system as far as I would have liked or should have. I defined the brand foundations, designed every component and pattern, and created product flows and prototypes for every feature. It was more than enough to get the product built and launched, but I didn't write any documentation. I should have.

Not to beat myself up too much; the annotated designs and style guides I

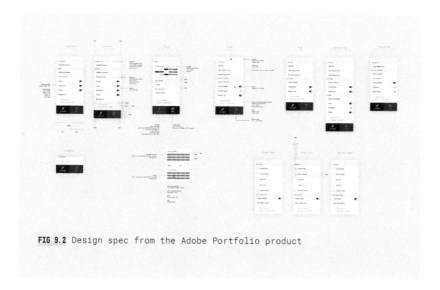

FIG 9.2 Design spec from the Adobe Portfolio product

created were very detailed. I even defined the CSS on them! But 'red-line' design specs aren't good enough. They're a form of documentation — sure — but they don't go into enough detail. These specs were more than enough to get the product into development, but they left a lot to interpretation on the design side — which wasn't enough for designers to work with in the future.

To demonstrate what I mean by 'red-line' design specs, FIG 9.2 is a spec I created for a "Remote" (in the Adobe Portfolio product).

I would describe FIG 9.2 — at best — as a style guide or spec for a design system pattern. It details every state and scenario. The text is tiny in the picture (as it's presented in this book), but take it from me: the annotations clearly define the sizes, spacing, and specifications. However, it leaves many unanswered questions:

- *Why* does it look like it does?
- Why a draggable remote versus a fixed menu item?
- *What* exactly does this pattern do?
- How does it respond to X scenario in the live product?
- What happens when I click the links versus the toggles?
- What happens if the remote is dragged off-screen?

None of the answers are obvious from the design alone. The above questions about logic, systematic design, and functionality don't just help designers understand how to work with the system, they also help developers build it! In fact, some of the bullet points above were real questions I was asked by developers working on this product with me.

Without documentation, we leave patterns like this open to interpretation. The next designer (or team of designers) who iterates on this pattern are going to have questions. With no answers to those questions, they will do their own thing, and the system that governed the original design will take a different path.

Similarly, the following image **(FIG 9.3)** shows button components from the same product.

9.1 airbnb.design/building-a-visual-language/

9.2 roomfive.net/adobe-portfolio/

FIG 9.3 A style guide for button components

This style guide specifies everything needed to build the component, but no information as to:

- Why are there different types of buttons?
- When and why should I use a blue button, versus a green button?
- When and why should I use a text link, versus a button?
- Can I pair the different colours and types of buttons together?
- Can we, and do we have guidelines for including icons in buttons?

I can tell you that — in this design system — the meaning behind the colours is important, and there very definitely are guidelines for when to use each type of button, and how they pair together. The logic for all of this should have been documented, or the original intent could be lost.

We are talking somewhat in ideals here. In reality, things don't always unfold as optimally as they should. For this particular project, time was very much a factor. I make my excuses, but this experience taught me a valuable lesson. What I should have done was to document the design system as it was being designed — as part of the design process, rather than waiting until a convenient time... Later... Or in this case never (I moved on from Adobe a couple months after this product's launch). This issue is, I'm sure, something most of you can relate to. Failing to document your design decisions is sometimes genuinely unavoidable. But often times we're just making excuses, and it costs our teams, products, and users down the road.

Document as you go

A good way to approach documentation is to think about what questions someone might have about what you (or your team) designed. There are no stupid questions, really. What's obvious to you might not be obvious to others. Get it all out of your head, and documented.

- Write guidelines that act as a source of truth, or reference material.
- Explain what 'it' is.
- When, where, why, and how do you use it?
- Document and/or demonstrate any functionality, animation, or conditional logic.
- Lead by example and show example use cases.
- Include as much detail as is appropriate. You can even include the code!

What should you document?

This is not a comprehensive list of everything you should document, but here are some basics to get you started:

Do's and don'ts

Throughout your documentation, it can be useful to give example use cases of how to do (or not do) something. As they say: 'a picture is worth a thousand words'. Seeing is believing. Showing an example scenario where your guidelines apply can be key to helping people understand context and application.

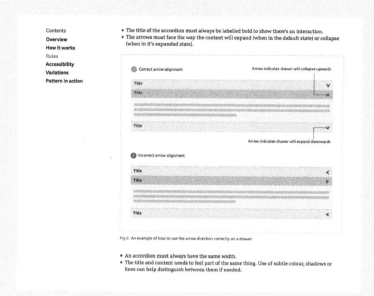

Contents
Overview
How it works
Rules
Accessibility
Variations
Pattern in action

- The title of the accordion must always be labelled bold to show there's an interaction.
- The arrows must face the way the content will expand (when in the default state) or collapse (when in it's expanded state).

Fig 6 An example of how to use the arrow direction correctly on a drawer

- An accordion must always have the same width.
- The title and content needs to feel part of the same thing. Use of subtle colour, shadows or lines can help distinguish between them if needed.

FIG 9.4 bbc.co.uk/gel/guidelines/accordion

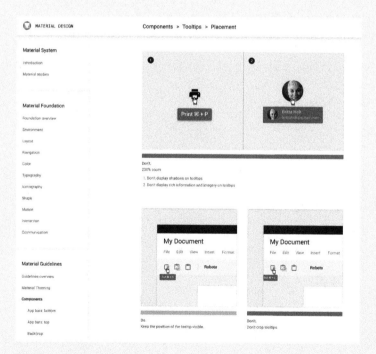

FIG 9.5 material.io/design/components/tooltips.html

The BBC example **(FIG 9.4)** simply uses a wireframe to demonstrate the correct and incorrect way of designing an accordion. The Google Material example **(FIG 9.5)** goes into more detail, using real scenarios from a product to demonstrate how tooltips should look and function.

Importantly: in both cases, the example use case imagery is accompanied by text explaining what's wrong or right about each approach. Don't assume your audience can identify right or wrong themselves — this is about *education*, it's not a test.

Colour

Don't just output a colour palette and hope people use it correctly. A swatch of colours (alone) can be used in a limitless number of ways. Write guidelines for:

- Why did you choose these brand colours?
- What is their intent? When and why would you use X colour over Y colour?
- Include useful information like its hex value (e.g. #b85c35) and its name.
- How do you reference a colour in the code?
- Show example use cases.

OpenTable specify each colour's name, hex value, a list of acceptable use cases for each colour, and even give insight into their thinking behind the colour. The more insight into the design decisions you give, the better the system's adopters will understand and apply the system. Referencing the OpenTable example **(FIG 9.6):**

> *"Early Girl is our star for experiences targeting our diners: the primary color in our corporate identity. Early girl conveys the energy and passion we invest in connecting our diners to new experiences and the warmth of great hospitality."*

> *"Blueberry is primarily used as a secondary action color. In our restaurant-focused marketing efforts, we focus on efficient service and streamlined reservation tools, and our blue is a calming assurance of our loyalty to business support."*

FIG 9.6 Primary brand colour palette

In contrast to OpenTable's primary brand colours **(FIG 9.6)** — and a more extensive secondary palette of equally bright colours — they also have a simple "Neutrals" palette **(FIG 9.7)**, intended mainly for headers and copy.

Here's how they describe this 'neutrals' palette:

> *"There are colors used for action and attention, while others are used for utility. These neutral colors are meant to pair well with the primary and secondary action colors and provide balance within the larger palette."*

Consistent and intentional use of colour is not only good for reinforcing a brand's identity and message – it also aids the user experience. For example, it's good practice to use prominent and consistent colours for calls to action in order to draw attention to them. If you use too many different colours for things like buttons and links, it becomes unclear what is actionable, and what isn't.

OpenTable's colour documentation defines acceptable use cases for each colour:

- Their secondary colour palette is *only* for use in background colours. *Not* calls to action, headers, or copy.
- The only colours used for calls to action (e.g. buttons and links) are their two primary colours.
- Their neutrals palette is used primarily for headers and copy — clearly distinguishing copy from calls to action.

FIG 9.7 brand.opentable.com/color/

Brand identity

Branding and logos can be a big investment of time and money, so protect your brand by documenting how it should be used. Some things to consider:

- Are there any guidelines for logo size?
- Can the logo overlay an image, or should it only be used on a plain background?
- Can the colours be changed? Can the logo be all white to use on a dark background, or all black to use on a light background?

The guidelines and decisions you make when designing a system are no good just in your head. They're not 'need to know'. Everyone on your team needs to know.

- What should we use for a Twitter avatar?
- Where do I find a vector download for this asset?

FIG 9.8 brand.opentable.com/logo/

To use another example **(FIG 9.8)** from OpenTable's digital brand guidelines: a nice touch here is that they include a rationale for why the logo looks the way it does. This may seem trivial to some, but the ethos behind their brand identity is core to the design of their companies services and products. Understanding this is key to working with their design system:

> *"With just a few shapes, our logo says a lot. It symbolizes the connection we forge between restaurants and diners, the way we help diners find the perfect fit, and the fact that our customers are always our focus."*

OpenTable's documentation for their logo is comprehensive. In addition to their rationalisation of the logos' design, they cover:

- Guidelines for the different ways it can be presented ("Lockups").
- The minimum size the various versions should be used.
- Guidelines on spacing.

- Do's and don'ts.
- A download of the digital assets.
- And as seen below **(FIG 9.9):** the "preferred treatment" of the logo, including what to do when that's not an option.

FIG 9.9 Preferred treatments of logo (example use cases)

Typography

Using a consistent and limited set of text styles, font-families, and font-weights simplifies the complexity of a user interface and lowers the cognitive load for the user. It also reduces the page load time, makes the text more legible, and reduces the amount of code required. As someone who's built many websites designed by other designers, I can tell you with confidence: sticking to a consistent range of text styles is something many designers fail to do.

For typefaces and font-weights:

- Limit the number of typefaces and font-weights you use.
- Note that the more typefaces (and different weights of fonts) you use, the slower your page will load, particularly for users on mobile phone/cellular networks. So consider this: do you need to use semi-bold *and* bold font-weights? Pick one.

Using a consistent and limited set of text styles, font families, and font weights simplifies the complexity of a user interface and lowers the cognitive load for the user.

- Define intent for each typeface. Why and when should you use typeface X over Y? For example, do you use a serif to distinguish headers and a sans-serif for copy?

For text styles:

- Aim to create a broad range of text styles that cover different scenarios. Don't just suggest a body text style and a headline text style, consider cases like subheaders, leading paragraphs, blockquotes, bulleted lists, image captions, and so on.
- You probably don't need a header text style in 19px *and* 20px font-size. Pick one.
- What does each text style look like?
- Document, at a minimum, each style's font-size, line-height, and letter-spacing.
- Do different header and copy styles have specific margins or padding?
- If appropriate, provide some context as to when to use each text style. Do you have a default size for copy? A particularly large or small text-size was likely created for a specific use case. If so, document that intent.

I like how Marvel's typography documentation **(FIG 9.10)** includes a little write-up on why they chose the typeface they did.

> *"Marvel's primary typeface is Fakt Soft Pro — a <u>robust</u> typeface with <u>legible numbers</u> that <u>renders well at all sizes</u>. It is soft and <u>friendly</u>, yet <u>plain</u> enough to get out of the way and let the user's designs shine."*

I like how BBC GEL document "Type in action" **(FIG 9.11)** — showing how and where to use different typefaces and text styles with simple wireframe examples.

Copywriting

Your brand likely has a tone of voice and a style to adhere to for copywriting; these guidelines will apply for all copy across your digital brand, whether it's marketing copy, headers, labels, or error messages. If everyone on your team writes their own copy 'as they speak', your brand won't have a unified voice, and won't communicate as effectively as it could. So be sure your documentation includes answers to questions such as:

- What is our brand's tone of voice? Is it assertive, friendly, bold, etc.?

FIG 9.10 marvelapp.com/styleguide/design/typography

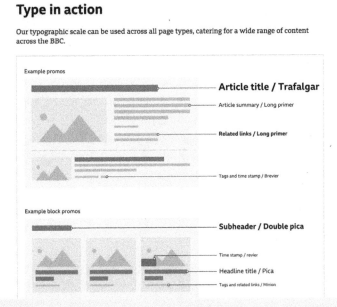

FIG 9.11 bbc.co.uk/gel/guidelines/typography

- What words do we use? Do we say "Hey!" or "Hello"? Do we say "employee" or "team member"?
- Do we use sentence case, or title case for headers?
- Do we include a period at the end of headers?
- How do we format date, time, and currency? Do we write "June 24, 1982" or "24th June, 1982"?
- Are we concerned about localisation/internationalisation?

For more tips on documenting copywriting, take a look back at the "Brand Tone of Voice and Copywriting" section in the "Laying the Foundations" chapter in this book.

Components

Components come in many sizes, shapes, colours, and types. Make sure you capture them all, plus all their variations and states. Some basic considerations for your documentation to get you started:

- Demonstrate what the component looks like, including all its different states (e.g. placeholder, value, hover, error, disabled).

FIG 9.12 primer.style/css/components/buttons

- Provide context as to why and when you would use the component.
- When should we use one type of button over another?
- Do form inputs need a placeholder?
- Do we hide or show labels above — or inline with — form inputs?

The Primer design system by GitHub has great documentation for their button components **(FIG 9.12)**. They have example live components you can interact with to really get a feel for how they work. They also show how to apply them in the code, and include a little write-up as to their use cases. This write-up is important, especially in cases like Primer where there are multiple types of buttons — as it provides context as to when to use each variant.

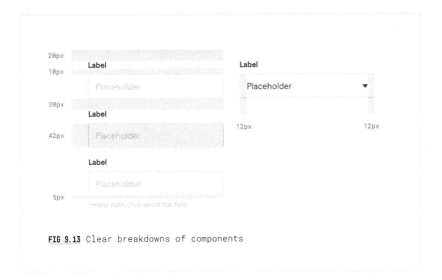

FIG 9.13 Clear breakdowns of components

The following two images are examples of text input **(FIG 9.14)** and button **(FIG 9.15)** component documentation I've created. Where the Primer documentation **(FIG 9.12)** is a living style guide — using dynamic, interactive components from production — I like to use (static) visuals to demonstrate all the different states of each component. This allows me to be more explicit as to their different states.

While live, interactive components are great, they do leave a lot to interpretation. With this in mind, perhaps it's worth doing both (include a live interactive component and a static mockup of all its states). Where static visuals require more work to maintain, they can be really valuable to foster understanding of how the component works, as they allow you to clearly demonstrate all the different states of the component (I'll discuss the pros and cons of using dynamic examples in your documentation later in this chapter.)

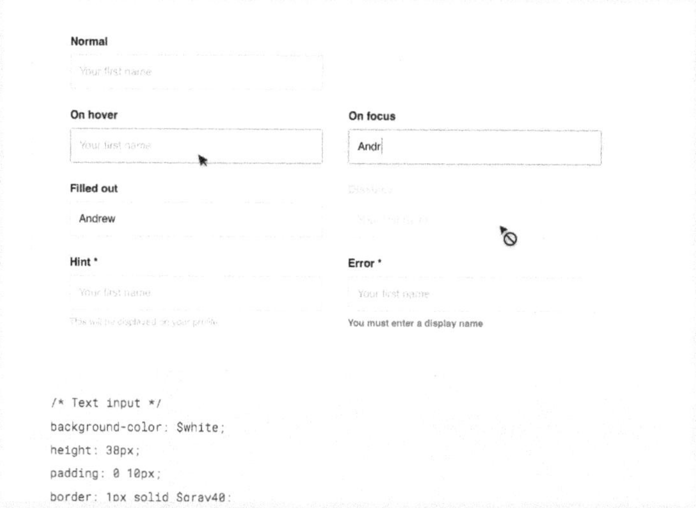

Normal

On hover

On focus

Andr

Filled out

Andrew

Hint *

Error *

You must enter a display name

```
/* Text input */
background-color: $white;
height: 38px;
padding: 0 10px;
border: 1px solid $grav40;
```

FIG 9.14 plasma.guide/form-specs/

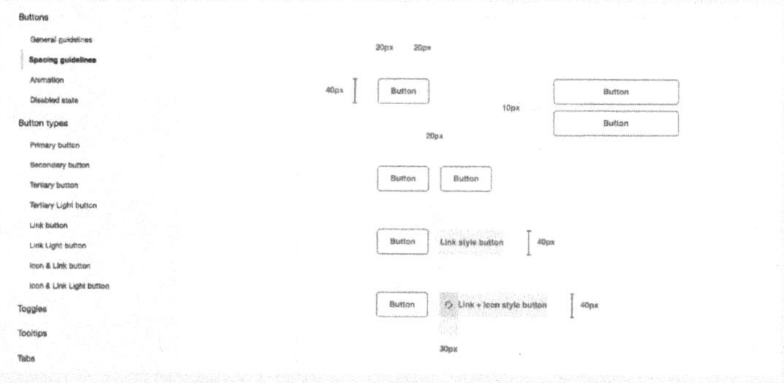

FIG 9.15 plasma.guide/buttons/

When documenting components, I also like to include the basic CSS; this allows me to be even more explicit about the component's makeup — plus I believe it's healthy for designers to be exposed to CSS and get a sense for how things are made **(FIG 9.14)**. I also include annotated breakdowns of the component **(FIG 9.13 + 9.15)**, and written guidelines of their makeup (e.g. spacing, sizes, and other specifications), and example use cases.

Atlassian do a nice job of annotating the makeup of their components **(FIG 9.16)** and patterns **(FIG 9.17)**:

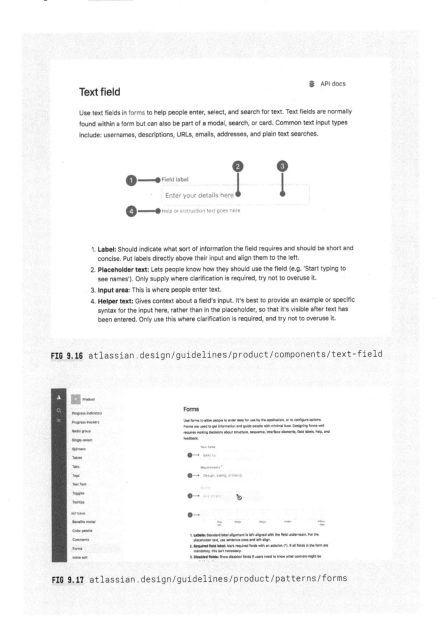

FIG 9.16 `atlassian.design/guidelines/product/components/text-field`

FIG 9.17 `atlassian.design/guidelines/product/patterns/forms`

Failing to document our design decisions is sometimes unavoidable. But often times we're just making excuses, and it costs our teams, products, and users down the road.

Patterns

Patterns are the larger building blocks of a user interface that are used repeatedly throughout a design. You should capture each of these patterns, and answer questions such as:

- Are our patterns modular? How do they work together?
- What is the purpose of each pattern?
- What are some example use cases?
- How does a pattern respond at different browser widths, and on different devices?
- Is there any conditional logic, or variants to suit different content scenarios?

BBC GEL does a really nice and very thorough job of documenting their design patterns (**FIG 9.18**); they explain the makeup of the pattern (**FIG 9.19**), what it is, when you could use it, any differences between iOS and Android (**FIG 9.20**), and include any rules and variations.

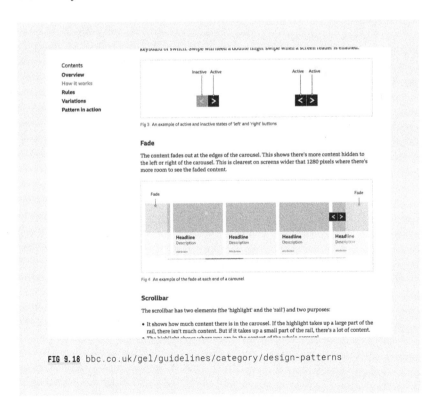

FIG 9.18 bbc.co.uk/gel/guidelines/category/design-patterns

They even include guidelines and designs for edge cases, such as:

- What happens if JavaScript is turned off? **(FIG 9.21)**
- How do patterns respond to long words in tight spaces? **(FIG 9.22)** They use the Welsh language as an example, but you could use German, or any long words in any language! Remember: use realistic (and unruly) content when you design.

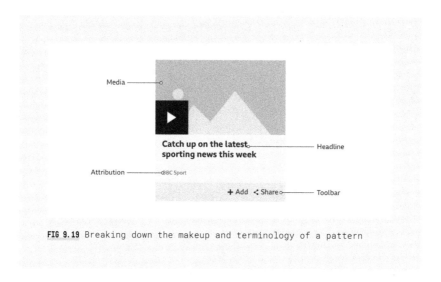

FIG 9.19 Breaking down the makeup and terminology of a pattern

Bootstrap also does a nice job of documenting patterns **(FIG 9.23)**; they lead with a description of the pattern (not seen in the screenshot, but visit the link), several interactive example variants of the pattern, and great CSS and JavaScript documentation. Documenting the code and use cases makes it easy to integrate the pattern into a project. **Design system documentation is for your whole team: designers *and* developers.**

Don't forget the small things

The obvious things to document are text styles, colours, buttons, and inputs — but don't forget components and patterns like avatars, pagination, tooltips, pills, toggles, loading spinners, breadcrumbs, and so on.

Marvel *(not that Marvel)* have a neat little section on how they present avatars **(FIG 9.24)**. It's smart that they have a fallback to the user's initials in the absence of an image. Empty states are an important thing to design for and document.

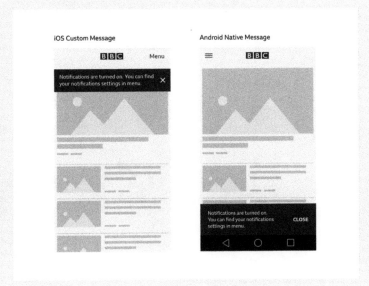

iOS Custom Message

Android Native Message

BBC Menu

Notifications are turned on. You can find your notifications settings in menu. ✕

≡ BBC

Notifications are turned on. You can find your notifications settings in menu. CLOSE

FIG 9.20 Pattern variants for iOS and Android

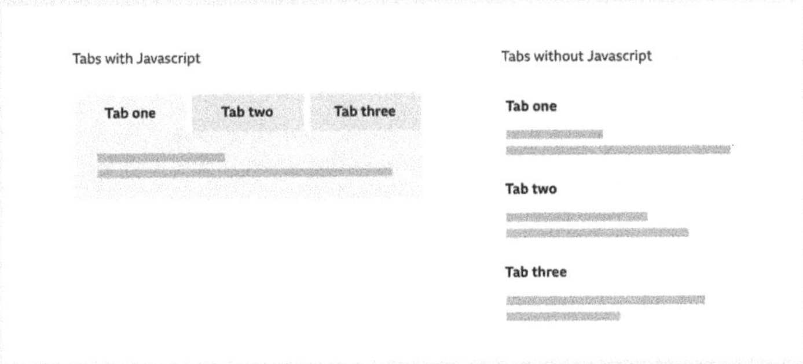

Tabs with Javascript

| Tab one | Tab two | Tab three |

Tabs without Javascript

Tab one

Tab two

Tab three

FIG 9.21 What happens when JavaScript is turned off?

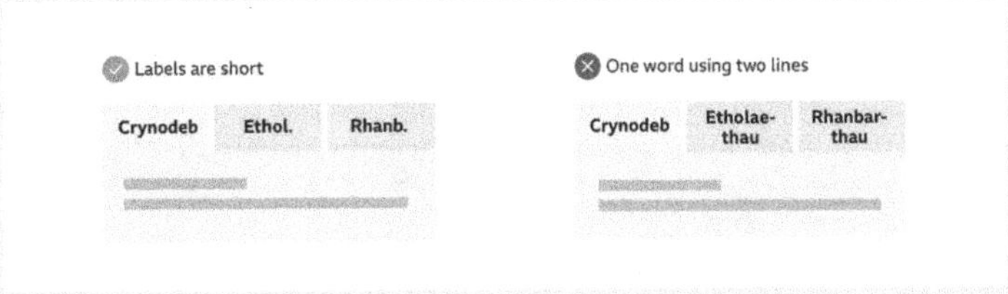

✓ Labels are short

| Crynodeb | Ethol. | Rhanb. |

✕ One word using two lines

| Crynodeb | Etholae-thau | Rhanbar-thau |

FIG 9.22 Do's and don'ts for dealing with long words

FIG 9.23 getbootstrap.com/docs/4.2/components/carousel/

Do you have a system philosophy covering how component and patterns are animated and loaded, what border radius or drop-shadows to use, and so on? If you do, document it. The Carbon design system by IBM has a section in their documentation on "Loading" **(FIG 9.25)**, including 'skeleton states' (load states used to illustrate the overall architecture of the page while it's loading), progressive loading, loading spinners, and so on.

Grid, layout, and spacing

It's all very well and good to design and document a mass of components and patterns, but they're effectively a UI kit without some logic for how they work together. Document the system accounting for things like:

- Is there consistent spacing in and around components and patterns?
- Are patterns designed to be modular?
- Is the design system responsive, or designed to a grid?
- How does the layout respond at different browser widths?
- Are there any considerations for designing for different devices?

BBC GEL do a great job of documenting their rationale and system thinking for grid, spacing, and layout **(FIG 9.26 + 9.27)**.

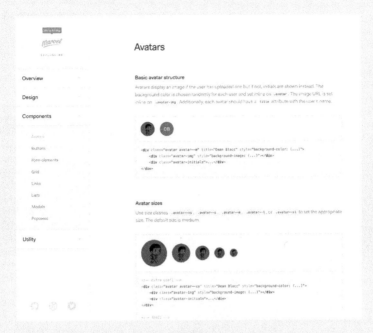

FIG 9.24 marvelapp.com/styleguide/components/avatars

FIG 9.25 carbondesignsystem.com/patterns/loading

Contents
Overview
Spacing and layout
Grid sizes
Considerations

Overview

We use a flexible grid that has percentage-based columns, fixed margins and gutters. The columns are used to adjust the layout, making the best use of the space available.

FIG 9.26 bbc.co.uk/gel/guidelines/grid

Contents
Overview
Spacing and layout
Grid sizes
Considerations

Spacing and layout

The grid uses fixed margins and gutters to help control the proportion and balance of the page. The margins and gutters are set to 8px for small screens and 16px for larger screens.

We change the sizes at different breakpoints to give the best possible layout for viewing our content.

For large screens we set the grid to a maximum width of 1280px, giving a content area of 1248px.

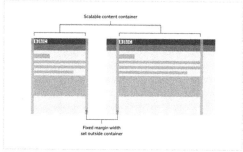

Fig 2 An example of how our container scales with fixed margins

Creating layouts

Any number of columns can be used to suit the content and create interesting layouts at different widths.

In the browser the columns will be built with percentages and will be 100% width by default. If required the percentage can be changed and columns can be introduced.

This provides a large amount of flexibility to suit the content on any device.

An example of this would be with an article page. On a large device, the main reading column could be sized at 60% and the supporting content can be placed in outer columns that are both sized at 20%. Providing a centralised reading experience with a suitable line-length.

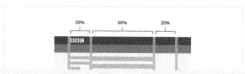

FIG 9.27 bbc.co.uk/gel/guidelines/grid

Look back at the "Responsive Design" section of the "Laying the Foundations" chapter in this book for more on responsive design.

Design tokens

We covered what design tokens are in the previous chapter. Suffice to say, if you have design tokens, your documentation definitely needs to include a source of truth for what they are and how to use them!

The Lightning design system documentation **(FIG 9.28)** does a good job of explaining what each design token is for. Without this context, the design tokens could be misused, and you could lose the advantages that come with creating them in the first place.

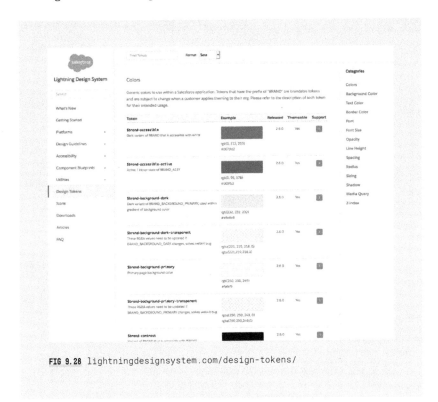

FIG 9.28 lightningdesignsystem.com/design-tokens/

How do you document a design system?

This is probably the most contentious part of this chapter. There are a multitude of ways you can do this, and there are dozens of tools and resources created specifically for this task! I won't get too into the technological depths of how to document a design system in this book, but you can find a list of great tools and resources on the website (9.3).

Since there are so many options available to you, you should discuss amongst your team what approach would be most effective for everyone. Developers are likely going to be key to these discussions, as they are better placed to set up an environment to write, edit, share, maintain, and publish the documentation.

The basic factors you need to address are:

- It needs to be accessible and editable by your team.
- It needs to be easily shareable and visible to all stakeholders.
- It can include text and images (visuals are important to aid understanding).
- It's likely going to be large, so it needs to be easy to navigate. And the navigation needs to be scalable, to grow as you add more to the system.

And the nice-to-haves are:

- Ability to include (or embed) live, interactive examples.
- Ability to include code snippets/examples.
- A changelog so you can track iterations to the system over time.
- Ability to search for content.

Getting started, the easy way

There's only one rule for how to document your design systems: *don't let technology or design bias stand in the way of progress.*

It's easy for a designer to get swept away in the presentation and styling of something, or get intimidated by technological barriers. Similarly, it's easy for a developer to get caught up in the most efficient or securest means of content managing, maintaining, and hosting the documentation. Both parties can be highly opinionated. Don't allow this friction to cause delay.

I felt this friction the first time I approached design system documentation.

9.3 designsystemfoundations.com/resources/

Don't leave documentation until the end, or as an afterthought. If you do, it might never get done. Make documentation part of your design and build process.

As a designer *and* a developer, I felt almost imprisoned by the multitude of options available! My initial goal — having seen so many stellar examples online — was to create a custom branded website to document the system. Thankfully, after a little research I quickly realised that the time spent thinking about, researching, designing, and building this website was only delaying me actually creating the documentation!

So to get started I simply created a new Google Doc **(9.4)** and started typing.

FIG 9.29 A screenshot from documentation I've created in Google Docs

As the document grew, I realised Google Docs covered all the basics (from the list earlier) of what we needed it to do.

- It's simple and fast to set up and write.
- It's easily accessible by your team.
- You can control privacy by setting who does and doesn't have access to it, and assign levels of access — such as read or comment only.
- Your team can comment inline, which is great for feedback and iteration.
- You can insert images and tables for visuals and example use cases.

9.4 google.com/docs/about/

214

- The 'Document Outline' feature — plus the ability to link/anchor to bookmarks and headings within the document — provides (good enough) navigation.

A Google Doc might not be the most exciting means of documentation, but it does provide an effective and fast means of documenting everything from foundations, such as copywriting, brand tone of voice, and formatting **(FIG 9.30):**

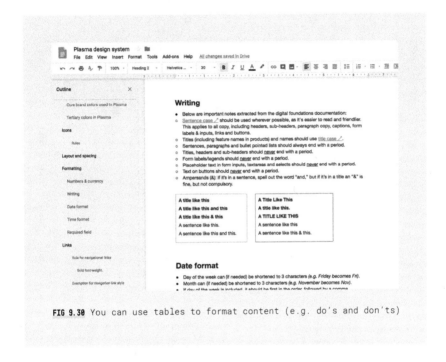

FIG 9.30 You can use tables to format content (e.g. do's and don'ts)

To documenting components **(FIG 9.31)** and patterns **(FIG 9.32).**

Note: These Google Doc example screenshots are from the Plasma design system. If you're interested, I wrote a case study **(9.5)** about the design and documentation of this system.

9.5 medium.com/owl-studios/plasma-design-system-4d63fb6c1afc

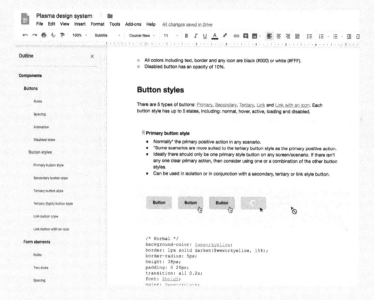

FIG 9.31 Documenting components

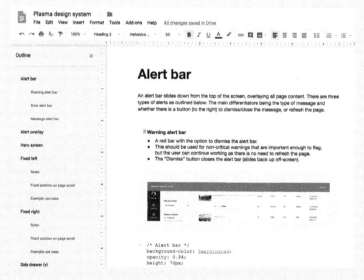

FIG 9.32 Documenting patterns

Google Docs is a genuinely good tool for documentation, but it only takes you so far. Where the Plasma design system was concerned, we did experience growing pains:

- It's inefficient to quickly link to specific content within the document (e.g. from Slack or an email).
- Searching for content could be easier.
- You can't embed live, interactive examples of components and patterns.
- And despite your best efforts to format the content 'nicely', a Google Doc isn't the most engaging way to present content (depending on your audience).

For what it's worth, this particular Google Doc did its job for nearly a year while we focussed on more pressing tasks, like actually building and implementing the system! *Don't lose sight of your priorities.*

In time, opportunities arose to evolve the documentation into more of a 'living style guide', which aimed to include live examples from production and code snippets, along with a more accessible, user-friendly, and branded user experience.

Living style guides

One of the bigger challenges of design systems is keeping the design, code, and documentation in sync. Consider these scenarios:

- A designer iterates on a button, the code and design library are updated, but the designer forgets to update the image mockup of the button in the static documentation.
- Similarly, if any code snippets (in the static documentation) are written as non-dynamic text entries, then they won't reflect any updates made to the production code, unless someone remembers to manually make the updates.

It's an easy mistake to make, but the documentation isn't of much use when it's different to the actual design system.

The key difference between a living style guide and static documentation is that a living style guide contains live design elements pulled directly from — or embedded from — the live source code. They are real and dynamic — not (only) an image or a mockup of a component. You can hover over a component and interact with it. And perhaps most importantly, they (somewhat automatically) evolve as your system evolves.

With a living style guide, any changes you make to production will be reflected in the documentation, at least where the live examples and code are concerned. Any write-up concerning the foundation, component, or pattern will still need to be updated.

Regardless of whether you choose to use static or dynamic documentation, the most important takeaway is this: **it should be part of your process to update anything in your documentation that's not automated** whenever you make changes to a design system.

If not a Google Doc, then what?

If you want to create more dynamic design system documentation — something more than a Google Doc — then there are a multitude of ways you can do it. There are also ways to generate living style guides directly from your code!

More and more tools and resources are being created all the time. As stated before; technology moves too fast for print, so rather than writing about them in this book — and risking tools becoming obsolete, or missing new tools post-publishing — I've linked to various tools and resources on this book's website **(9.6)**.

Spinning up editable documentation and living style guides enters developer territory — or at least an area where designers and developers should converge. Since this is a design-focussed book, my advice is to speak to the developers on your team and tell them you want to create design system documentation (or the Digital Foundations we spoke about earlier in this book). Don't be afraid to ask. My experience has often been that experts will appreciate you seeking their help.

Tell the developers you need:

- A platform the whole team can contribute to and update on a regular basis.
- The ability to write and format text and upload images.

9.6 designsystemfoundations.com/resources/

9.7 gitbook.com

9.8 wikipedia.org/wiki/Markdown

9.9 github.com

- The ability to add new pages and organise content by sections and subsections.
- A simple navigation which scales when you add new content.
- The ability to pull in or embed real components and patterns from production (code) to demonstrate design system elements.
- To publish the documentation online (publicly), or — if you prefer it be private — to make it password protected.

Note: The above list isn't comprehensive, it's just to get you started. I advise that you get together with your team to discuss the best solutions to benefit all parties.

For what it's worth, in the Plasma design system example earlier — where we moved from static documentation in Google Docs to a more dynamic solution — we used a tool called GitBook **(9.7)**.

The basic premise of GitBook is this: you write your documentation in markdown **(9.8)** (a simple formatting language) in GitHub **(9.9)**, then GitBook weaves its magic to convert it into a website. Full disclosure: I'm a front-end developer and I still struggled to get this set up on my own, so I worked with developers on our team to get it all running — I advise you to do the same. Once it was set up, it was easy to write the documentation in markdown (once you get used to it), and you need only a basic understanding of HTML and CSS to customise the style of the site and tailor the documentation to your brand.

Don't worry if creating a dynamic documentation website sounds too challenging for now! As I said, using a simple tool like Google Docs for your design system documentation will take you far, and is much better than not documenting at all.

We've covered a lot in this chapter! Let's take the foot off the pedal and look at some inspiration for documenting design systems in the next chapter.

GALL—
ERY

10

In the "Laying the Foundations" chapter of this book, we talked about companies building public websites to show off their digital brand guidelines. More and more, it's becoming common practice for companies to make their brand guidelines and design system documentation public. Designers and developers are publicly opening up about their code, processes, and design thinking.

The great thing about these companies sharing their documentation publicly is that we can learn from them! Building on the examples I've included throughout this book, this chapter is a curation of great examples for you to explore, and includes a little insight into what makes them such good examples.

FIG 10.1 culture.basicagency.com

How a company presents its Digital Foundations and/or design system documentation in public — and the insights they provide into their design and engineering practices — says a lot about their culture. This in itself is a big part of the reason why presenting your work in the open is good — if nothing else, it helps you recruit the best talent.

Basic Culture

The Basic Culture Manual website **(FIG 10.1)** is a first-class example of a company flexing its muscles, giving an insight into their culture (quite literally in this case), and sending a firm message that: 'We make cool shit! Hire us. Work with us.'

We looked at Basic's website earlier in this book as a great example of documenting mission, values, and principles in the "Laying the Foundations" chapter. Their website is well worth a visit — if only to admire the design and animation — and be inspired by their values and design philosophies (FIG 10.2). There's something in here for everybody.

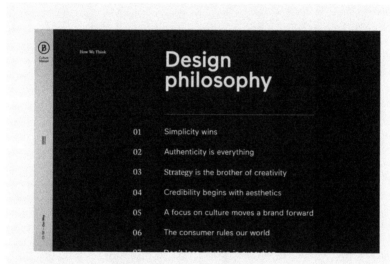

FIG 10.2 culture.basicagency.com/our-way

BBC GEL (Global Experience Language)

If you only look at one website for inspiration, look at the BBC GEL website (10.1). It includes more or less everything we covered in the "Document Everything" and "Laying the Foundations" chapters. GEL is a collection of digital brand guidelines, design system documentation, and articles on everything from "How to design for the (responsive) web", to interviews with their creative teams. It's even built into the chrome of the core BBC website; it's not a standalone website, so it all feels very inclusive and well-thought out.

Their "Foundations" section covers things like typography, grid, layout, spacing, and iconography. Their "Design Patterns" section (FIG 10.3) has detailed breakdowns of established patterns (like accordions, cards, and carousels) used throughout their digital properties, filtered by 'Web' and 'App'. Note: notice how each pattern shows whether there's a recent update to a pattern, and the date it was last updated:

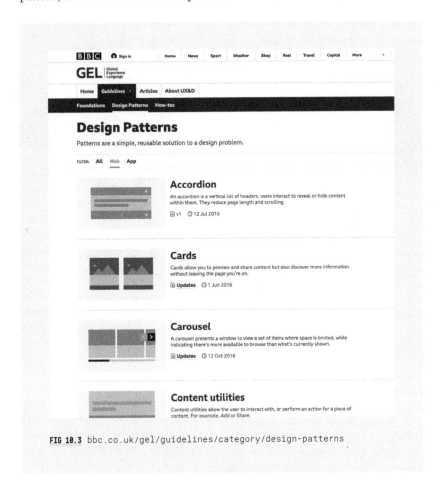

FIG 10.3 bbc.co.uk/gel/guidelines/category/design-patterns

One of the things I love most about GEL is how all of their documentation reads more like an article than documentation (FIG 10.4). It's well laid out and presented, and the content is inviting, easy to navigate and consume. Each page — whether it's a "how-to" article, or documentation governing typography or patterns — is clearly introduced with an easy to digest overview, the latest update, and the team that contributed to the system element or editorial. Any relevant downloads or links to the code are clearly visible, and each page has a sub-navigation, which is fixed on-scroll allowing you to skip-to important

FIG 10.4 bbc.co.uk/gel/guidelines/category/foundations

content, so you can find what you're looking for quickly.

What I find particularly great is their section of "How-to" articles (**FIG 10.5**). This clearly demonstrates a level of care and responsibility that all designers and engineers should aspire to. To quote from their "How to Design for Accessibility" article (**10.2**):

> *"We want the things we make to work for the whole audience, because the BBC believes everyone deserves the best. Our audience is diverse, not only in gender, age, and culture, but also in the ways they interact with us and the abilities they have to do so. To deliver an inclusive experience, accessibility must be an integral part of the user experience design. It must also be integral to development and testing."*

The BBC's design system documentation and digital brand guidelines are not just a technical blueprint, they are also thoughtful and inspirational, and give their teams a mission.

FIG 10.5 bbc.co.uk/gel/guidelines/category/how-to

It's interesting to note that the entire BBC GEL website is black and white. Colour is seldom used. Even the visuals focus heavily on wireframes to demonstrate their design system patterns — like the following example screenshot **(FIG 10.6)** showing a variant on their "Cards" pattern.

This is worth noting because by focusing more on structure than style, they are highlighting that their system foundations and patterns are really just a vehicle for their content. As we covered earlier in this book: **design for the content, don't fit the content to the design.**

FIG 10.6 Visuals focus on the pattern's makeup, not visual design

The BBC's patterns make no assumptions about the content. Given the abundance and wide range of content the BBC's various digital properties cover, it's imperative that **their patterns are designed to work with any content, not just best case scenarios.** And their documentation is a testament to that. They don't rely on 'pretty' visuals for them to work. They include long headlines, as opposed to convenient character counts. Patterns have variants to cover different scenarios, media, and content **(FIG 10.7)**. And they are all designed with accessibility in mind.

10.1 bbc.co.uk/gel/

10.2 bbc.co.uk/gel/guidelines/how-to-design-for-accessibility

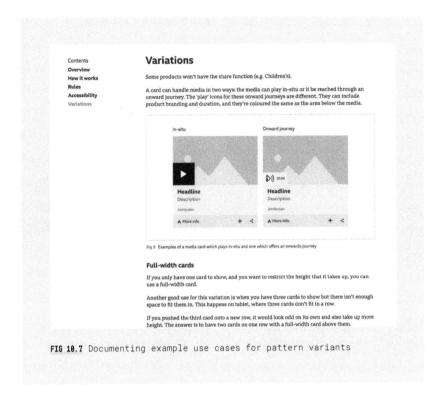

Contents
Overview
How it works
Rules
Accessibility
Variations

Variations

Some products won't have the share function (e.g. Children's).

A card can handle media in two ways: the media can play in-situ or it be reached through an onward journey. The 'play' icons for these onward journeys are different. They can include product branding and duration, and they're coloured the same as the area below the media.

In-situ

Onward journey

Headline
Description
Attribution

∧ More info   +   <

Headline
Description
Attribution

∧ More info   +   <

Fig 9   Examples of a media card which plays in-situ and one which offers an onwards journey

Full-width cards

If you only have one card to show, and you want to restrict the height that it takes up, you can use a full-width card.

Another good use for this variation is when you have three cards to show but there isn't enough space to fit them in. This happens on tablet, where three cards don't fit in a row.

If you pushed the third card onto a new row, it would look odd on its own and also take up more height. The answer is to have two cards on one row with a full-width card above them.

FIG 10.7 Documenting example use cases for pattern variants

The BBC's documentation shares more or less everything related to the design of their systems, even including some code. In contrast, Airbnb takes a very different approach.

Airbnb Design

Airbnb's public design system content shows that you can create buzz around your design system without actually making your system or its documentation public. Their "Airbnb Design" website **(FIG 10.8)** clearly demonstrates their strong design and engineering cultures, and the work that goes into creating their design systems. Their website features designers and engineers giving insight into their design process via articles, events, and case studies. It doesn't give much away in terms of the system or documentation itself, but it's an interesting insight into how they think about and design products and systems.

Articles   Events   Videos   Projects   Q

Articles

Explore our community features, case studies, opinion pieces, and more

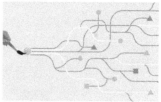

Building a Visual Language Behind the scenes of our new design system

Behind the Scenes

Painting with Code Introducing our new open source library React Sketch.app

Behind the Scenes, Projects

Ciao! Bonjour! Hello! Kon'nichiwa! Crafting global content that travels with you

Case Study, Perspectives

Working Type How we introduced Airbnb Cereal to our UI

Case Study, Projects

FIG 10.8 airbnb.design

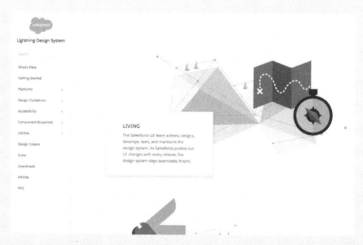

FIG 10.9 lightningdesignsystem.com

Lightning design system (Salesforce)

The Lightning design system documentation **(FIG 10.9)** is a treasure trove of knowledge. They even have a download section where you can download a comprehensive Sketch file of all the components and icons they use, and they even offer their pre-built CSS framework!

The Lightning documentation is very much a 'living style guide'; much of what you see is pulled directly from source, so you can interact with the system components and patterns.

Their system relies heavily on design tokens, which is reinforced throughout their documentation. They also include notes on the accessibility features of certain components, which is a nice touch — both because it educates us, and shows they care about all their users! Code is also featured throughout, including release notes, giving you in-depth insight into how to design and build with the system.

Where some documentation is aimed solely at designers, Lightning is very much aimed at designers and developers, or designer-developer hybrids.

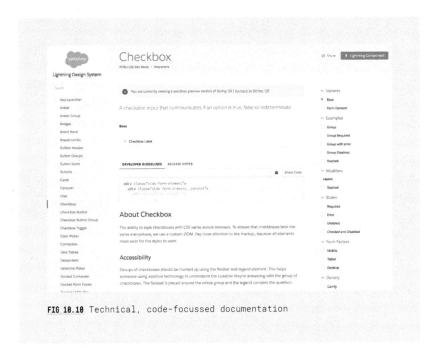

FIG 10.10 Technical, code-focussed documentation

It's all very well and good to design and document a mass of components and patterns, but they're effectively a UI kit without some logic for how they work together.

Where Salesforce's Lightning documentation is very much a living style guide, in contrast, the Nachos design system is more of a static style guide.

Nachos design system (Trello)

I like how simple and on-point the Nachos documentation website is. Trello's design documentation uses static images to showcase components, and that's fine, so long as the team responsible for maintaining the documentation updates those images when any changes are made to their appearance. Documenting systems in this way also requires less development support, so is arguably a more designer-friendly approach.

I love how detailed Trello gets with their image specs; this (for me) is something that makes (some) static documentation websites better than (some) living style guides. Interactive components are great, but I would still advise including some kind of specs to really highlight what goes into the creation of components and patterns. This way, **designers learn how it's made, and don't just see the end result.**

FIG 10.11 RIP Nachos website (formerly at: design.trello.com)

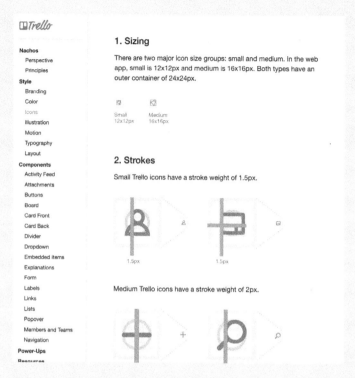

FIG 10.12 Documenting the anatomy of design elements

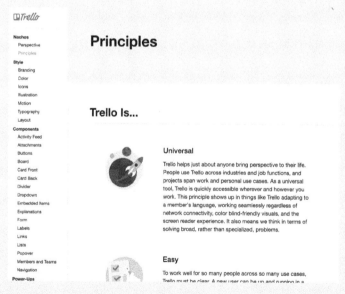

FIG 10.13 Design principles and design systems go hand-in-hand

Breaking down the anatomy of how a button is designed **(FIG 10.11)** — or how icons are created and what size they should be **(FIG 10.12)** — is both interesting and insightful, whether you're a member of the team using the design system, or an outsider admiring their work. Remember the note earlier on insight into culture... Well, the attention to detail Trello's documentation demonstrates is inspiring.

I also like that Trello have included their design principles **(FIG 10.13)** in with their documentation. In an ideal world, these things are inseparable. It's arguably 'odd' that so many design system documentation websites leave principles out (or don't have any).

Marvel design system

Dare I say it... Some design system documentation is plain ugly! Marvel's documentation **(FIG 10.14)** is a breath of fresh air with its clean and simple interface and presentation.

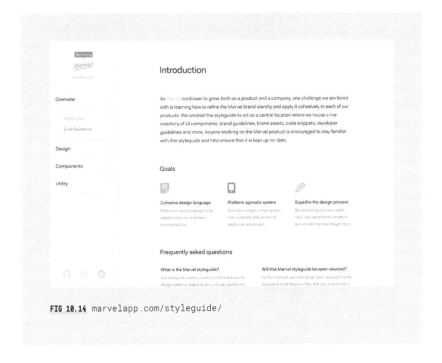

FIG 10.14 marvelapp.com/styleguide/

Their documentation home page is inviting and clear as to what you're looking at; it also includes its purpose and mission:

"We created this style guide to act as a central location where we house a live inventory of UI components, brand guidelines, brand assets, code snippets, developer guidelines, and more. Anyone working on the Marvel product is encouraged to stay familiar with this style guide and help ensure that it is kept up-to-date."

Notice the orange "We're hiring" prompt above their logo **(FIG 10.14)**... Recruitment is a key motivation for publicising a good deal of documentation websites — so why not make it obvious? If I was looking for a job with a company that cared about system design, I'd click that link.

Talking of 'pretty websites' (and flagging that we're hiring)... Damn, Primer, look at you **(FIG 10.15)**:

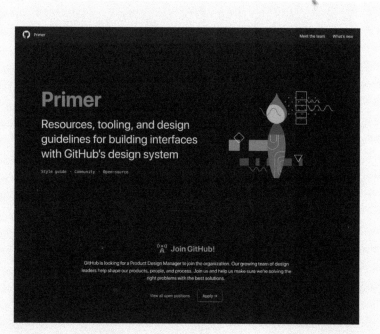

FIG 10.15 primer.style

The better your documentation is designed and the easier the content is to navigate, the more likely your team is to engage with it! Especially designers.

Primer design system (GitHub)

Similar to Marvel — only more pronounced this time — is GitHub's reference to recruitment, proudly and prominently presented in this beautifully designed gateway page to their design system documentation. Sexy design is certainly not the objective of design system documentation — don't get me wrong — but if you're going to all the trouble of creating this documentation, why not also make it look great. *The better it's designed and the easier the content is to navigate, the more likely your team is to engage with it!*

Carbon design system (IBM)

I like how Carbon splits its documentation of components into "Usage" (FIG 10.16) and "Code" (FIG 10.17). It's interesting to note their specificity over how and when to use a link or a button, and the limit for how many times a

FIG 10.16 carbondesignsystem.com/components/button/usage

primary button should be used on a page. I particularly like their breakdown of each button types' purpose:

> *"Buttons are used primarily on action items. Some examples include Add, Save, Delete, Sign up. Do not use Buttons as navigational elements. Instead, use Links because it takes the user to a new page and is not associated with an action. Each page may have one to two primary buttons. Any remaining calls-to-action are represented as secondary buttons."*

It's also helpful that, alongside their code documentation for each component, they include a link out to CodePen where you can view and edit the code **(10.3)**. I think this is a great idea, as it gives you the opportunity to play with the code so you can really understand how it works. This also helps to bridge the gap between design and development.

FIG 10.17 carbondesignsystem.com/components/button/code

10.3 codepen.io/team/carbon/pen/xeZxLe

Seeds (Sprout Social)

I really like how Sprout Social presents their brand guidelines and design system documentation in one central hub (FIG 10.18). I've stressed the importance of having a source of truth, and utilising digital brand guidelines as the foundations of products and design systems. Keeping everything together makes perfect sense. They *should* work together, so *why* separate them?

Seed's home page introduces what their "Creative Hub" is and why it's

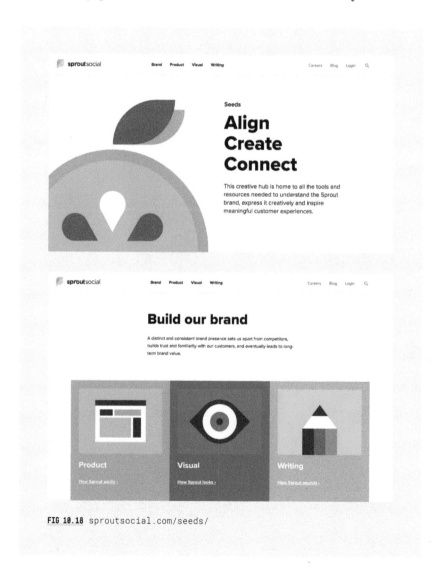

FIG 10.18 sproutsocial.com/seeds/

important, and a simple navigation at the top breaks the content into "Brand", "Product", "Visual", and "Writing". Love it. It also has a page with downloads, so their brand assets are easily accessible.

> *"A distinct and consistent brand presence sets us apart from competitors, builds trust and familiarity with our customers, and eventually leads to long-term brand value."*

I'm glad I found an example of a company who has chosen to protect some of it's design system content (**FIG 10.19**). Not everything needs to be for the public's eyes — some content is sensitive, or you may just prefer not to share it so openly. That's totally fine, but you want to be sure you're maintaining your single source of truth, rather than have public content 'here' and private content 'there'. Password protecting content that's for personnel eyes only is a simple solution.

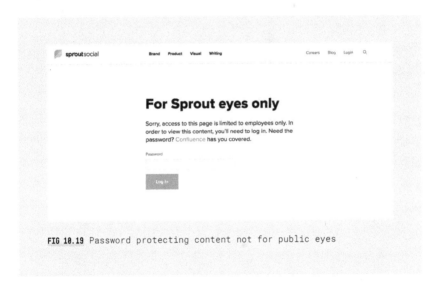

FIG 10.19 Password protecting content not for public eyes

Solid design system (BuzzFeed)

It's a good idea to keep your team informed about any changes being made to the design system they're working with. This is often referred to as a "Changelog", but in our example (**FIG 10.20**), BuzzFeed has a page called "Release Notes". This is where they document any updates: from changes to colour hex codes to pixel value changes to a border-radius, the addition of a new design token, or an update to a CSS class name or Sass variable, and so on.

FIG 10.20 solid.buzzfeed.com/release-notes.html

FIG 10.21 thumbprint.design/guide/product/color/

10.4 designsystemfoundations.com/resources/

10.5 @andrewcouldwell

Thumbprint design system (Thumbtack)

Thumbprint has a great "Guidelines" section in their documentation; it makes everything a little clearer for the system's adopters. Within 'Guidelines' there is a section on colour (FIG 10.21), which has nice do's and don'ts for each colour.

Moving on

It's my hope that the examples in this chapter have given you a sense of the range of possibilities and best practices for presenting Digital Foundations and design system documentation, or even giving insight into your company's design and engineering cultures.

I've done my best to curate the finest examples being shared today. However, there are so many more great examples out there, and new design system and documentation websites are popping up all the time — so be sure to check out this book's website (10.4) to get even more inspiration! And please share (10.5) any great examples you find.

Next up, we'll talk about one of the most difficult — but arguably most vital — parts of design system work: maintaining a design system.

MAIN— TAIN— ING A DESIGN SYSTEM

11

Congratulations, you've designed, documented, built, and integrated a design system! *(Or let's assume you have)*. Now for the bad news: that was the easy part! Keeping the design, code, and documentation in sync is arguably the most challenging part of working with design systems.

The following scenarios all lead to a design system's demise:

- Designers update their mockups, style guides, library, etc., but for whatever reason, the developers miss the changes — or they never get around to them — and the design changes don't get implemented in the code.
- Team members save work on their desktop or personal computers, as opposed to a shared team drive/location.
- Designers use their own personal set of foundations, components, and patterns, as opposed to a shared team library.
- The design and code is updated, but the documentation isn't.
- Team members use different (incompatible) tools and/or software.
- Teams aren't kept in the loop about changes to the design system.
- Team members feel excluded when they don't feel involved in — or have any opportunities to influence — the design or evolution of the system.

All of the above scenarios lead to the same outcome: designers work with one or more alternate versions of the design system, while developers work with the actual live version of the design system. This is frustrating for all parties — it's also completely avoidable.

Maintaining a design system requires **communication**, **process**, **teamwork**, **discipline**, and **stewardship**. In the sections to follow, we're going to look at how to achieve this, and solutions to all of the problem scenarios listed above.

Work with shared design assets

We covered the importance of setting up editable and responsive components, patterns, and foundations in the "Systematising the Design" chapter. We talked briefly about having them be easily accessible by your whole team. In this section I want to build on this and stress the importance of having a shared library of assets that your design team can simply insert into their designs. They should also be made aware of — and able to sync — any changes made to those assets.

When design teams work with shared assets, it ensures consistency and cuts down on unintentional design discrepancies. I think a shared library of design assets is the real game changer part of design systems — it's where much of the speed, ease, and efficiency comes in (at least on the design side of things).

I'm going to break my own rule concerning talking about tools in this book and recommend Sketch **(11.1)** for web and product designers working with teams of other designers. This is only going on my experience. I also recommend you try other tools and see what works best for your team. I've linked to some of these tools on this book's website **(11.2)**. But as a working example in this book, I'll use Sketch for demonstration purposes.

Using Sketch Library **(11.3)**, you can create a master design system file containing all design system foundations, components **(FIG 11.1 + 11.2)**, and patterns and save it somewhere accessible by all your team. It needs to be somewhere that will automatically sync any changes (e.g. Dropbox **11.4**).

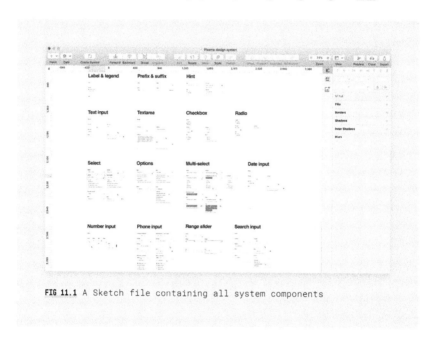

FIG 11.1 A Sketch file containing all system components

With your master design system file in a shared location, designers on your team can very simply and quickly insert assets from the master file into their

11.1 sketch.com

11.2 designsystemfoundations.com/resources/

11.3 sketch.com/docs/libraries/

11.4 dropbox.com

11.5 skl.sh/2xWBObZ

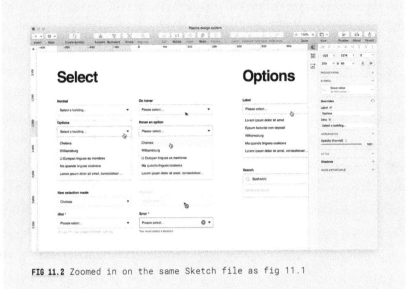

FIG 11.2 Zoomed in on the same Sketch file as fig 11.1

own design files. Then, any updates made to the master file will sync to any design files using its assets.

Don't worry if this sounds difficult — it's not — it's actually really fast and easy to set up! I've created a Skillshare class (**11.5**) demonstrating how to set up editable design system components and a Sketch Library.

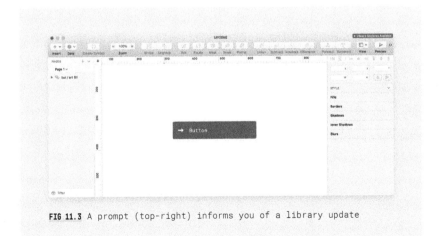

FIG 11.3 A prompt (top-right) informs you of a library update

If your team decides to change the colour of a button, it would be as simple as updating the button symbol in the master design system library file. In Sketch, the next time a member of your team is working on a design mockup, which uses this button they will see a "Library Updates Available" prompt to the top-right of their screen **(FIG 11.3)** letting them know there's been an update to a design asset they are using.

Clicking the "Library Updates Available" prompt opens up a convenient before and after ("Old" and "New") view of everything that has an update **(FIG 11.4)**. It might not always be appropriate to update, so it's good you get the choice so you can visually compare the change to measure what impact it will have on your design.

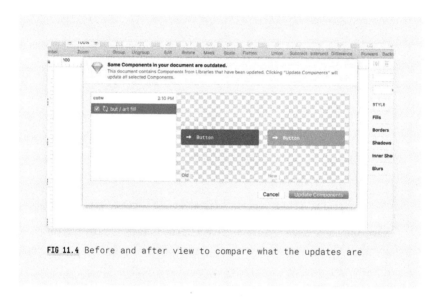

FIG 11.4 Before and after view to compare what the updates are

Working with patterns

While Sketch symbols and Sketch Library work very well for things like components, they don't (always) work so well for more complex elements like patterns. (At least, not yet — I'm sure as design tools continue to evolve, they will handle more complex patterns and responsive design better).

For patterns which are too complex to work as editable (Sketch) symbols accessed via Sketch Library, I recommend creating individual design files for each pattern and saving them somewhere easily accessible by your team. Again, this needs to be somewhere your team can easily sync updates or access the latest version of the file. In the below example's case **(FIG 11.5)**, I stored pattern files in a folder on Dropbox:

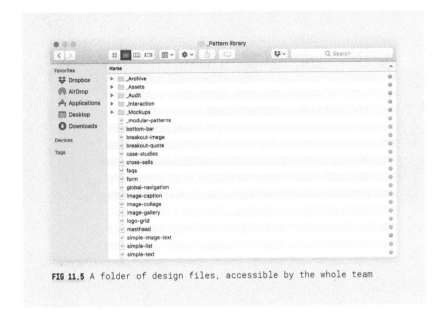

FIG 11.5 A folder of design files, accessible by the whole team

Each pattern's design file contains an up-to-date version of the pattern. If you're designing for the web, it helps to include responsive 'versions' of the pattern showing how it appears at different breakpoints. Setting up your patterns like this — ready to copy and paste into your designs — allows for rapid prototyping, and acts as a good source of truth for working with design system patterns.

The following screenshot **(FIG 11.6)** shows a responsive pattern in Sketch. You can see the desktop version of the pattern to the left, and to the right you see a hint of how the pattern appears at different breakpoints (e.g. tablet and mobile).

Designers can also refer to the documentation for the pattern to see visuals, a write-up, guidelines, and use cases **(FIG 11.7)**. Documentation can play a key role in maintaining a design system, as it provides a 'system of record' for how system elements are intended to be used.

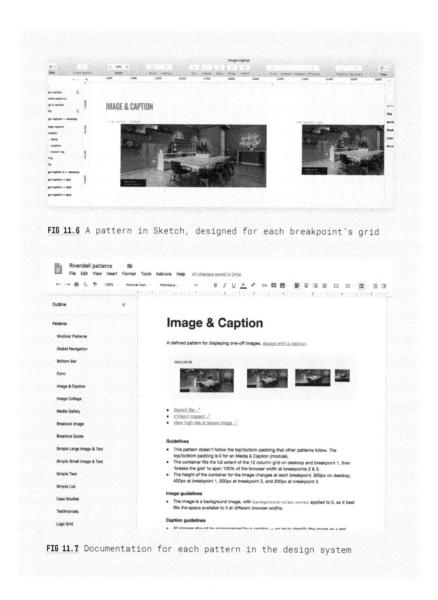

FIG 11.6 A pattern in Sketch, designed for each breakpoint's grid

FIG 11.7 Documentation for each pattern in the design system

Keep documentation up to date

We've covered documenting design systems extensively in this book, but for the sake of this chapter it's worth reiterating the importance of keeping your documentation up to date. Your documentation isn't of much use if it's recording a previous state or version of the design and/or code.

Your documentation should be a source of truth. When your team debates how something should look or work, the documentation is the place they will look for the answer — *assuming you did due diligence and documented your design thinking when you designed the foundation, component, or pattern in question.* **Make it a part of your process to update design and code documentation** when you create new — or update existing — system elements.

While design documentation updates are more of a manual process, it is possible to (at least somewhat) automate the process of code documentation. You can use dynamic documentation or living style guides that pull-in code from production, or documentation that's generated directly from the code (with varying degrees of success).

As this is a design-focussed book — and code documentation is outside my area of expertise — I'll leave the documentation of code to the experts (i.e. your engineering team). There are also links to some design system documentation tools and resources on this book's website **(11.6)**.

Keeping the design and code in sync

A problem every team faces with design systems is keeping the design and code in sync. It's difficult! When your team is designing with components that don't exist in your live product, it's easy for design systems to split into two versions:

1. The version designers work with.
2. The (real) version that the public sees, and that the developers work with.

Frustrated by having to keep Sketch files up to date and in-sync with the live version of their design system components, Airbnb sought to bridge the gap between design and code. They did this by experimenting with — and creating — an open-source library that allows you to write React **(11.7)** components that render to Sketch documents. This effectively allows designers and engineers to 'design in the browser', working with real data, APIs, and Flexbox **(11.8)**.

> *"In Sketch, we use symbols and overrides. In React, we use components and properties. The concepts are so similar that it seemed silly not to unify them."*

11.6 designsystemfoundations.com/resources/

11.7 reactjs.org

11.8 css-tricks.com/snippets/css/a-guide-to-flexbox/

Make it part of your process to update design libraries and any documentation when you create new, or update existing design system elements.

See Airbnb's *Painting with Code* article **(11.9)** by Design Technologist, Jon Gold **(11.10)** for more about this experiment.

Of course, methods like Airbnb's require designers on your team to have at least a basic understanding of coding languages like React and CSS, which is understandably a barrier to entry for most design teams.

More realistically speaking: keeping the design and code in sync comes down to process and discipline.

Here's the process — if you update the design of an existing system element, or add a new one, you should:

1. Update the library, style guide(s), or whatever design file(s) your team uses to share design assets.
2. Make sure the update is effectively tracked and queued for a developer to update the code, (for example, by creating a Github Issue).
3. Update any documentation.
4. Inform your team about the change. Ideally, they should be aware of the change before it's been made. If you include them in the process of figuring out why the change is needed and what the change should be, you will avoid any conflicts or repetition of work.

It's advisable to assign responsibilities within your team to make sure the above process is adhered to. We'll talk about design system guardians, ambassadors, teams, and leaders later in this chapter.

Code as a design tool

The line between traditional design tools and code is becoming blurred. A good number of design tools output CSS code of variable quality, and some design tools even allow you to insert React components from production into your designs. I'm sure this line will continue to blur as design tools become more advanced.

11.9 airbnb.design/painting-with-code/

11.10 jon.gold

Airbnb's Head of Design, Alex Schleifer (11.11) comments:

> *"We're investing in code as a design tool. Moving closer to working with assets that don't only include layout and design, but also logic and data. This helps bridge the gap between engineers and designers, thus reducing the need for design specs – or redlines – and the steps between vision and reality."*

Granting designers access to code may seem like a scary proposition to some. But consider the time designers spend waiting for developers to make changes, or the distraction developers feel when designers regularly want to make small tweaks. Maybe it's not such a crazy notion that designers could just work directly in the code?

The line between designer and developer is blurred at GitHub (11.12), which is hardly surprising given the nature of their business. Diana Mounter (11.13), a design system leader at GitHub, explains the benefit of designers writing code:

> *"Product designers and web designers at GitHub contribute production code and often assist in implementing their own designs. Some designers get deeper into the stack, but every product and web designer writes CSS. This means designers are primary users of Primer, our design system, and are often the first to notice when there are problems with styles or gaps in documentation."*

Keep your team in the loop

When you make updates to a design system, or even just while you are deliberating about updates, it's good practice to involve your team. This can mean a few things:

1. Meet as a team to discuss proposed changes to the system, as opposed to having individuals make updates that the team might not agree with, or aren't aware of.

11.11 twitter.com/alexoid

11.12 medium.com/@broccolini/design-systems-at-github-c8e5378d2542

11.13 broccolini.net

2. Keep a changelog so team members can see what's been updated, why the change was made, and when it changed.
3. Update the team when changes are made so people are kept in-the-know. A meeting is good, but people can be absent from meetings, and meetings don't always work well for remote teams, so consider something more inclusive — like sending an email, or writing a journal, post, or log of release notes — that detail the changes.
4. You could have a Slack channel dedicated to questions and updates related to the design system.
5. You could hold 'office hours', where members of the team — or a design system lead — are available to anybody who wishes to discuss anything about the system.
6. Use a task tracking tool like GitHub Issues, Trello, or Jira so people can post requests and bugs, or ask questions.

To quote from the same GitHub article as earlier:

> *"We started using team posts to tell people about new Primer [design system] updates, to give people a heads up when we shipped large code changes, and share more information behind our decisions."*

It's interesting to note that GitHub wanted to *"share more information behind our decisions"*. Providing context is always important in design systems. Context helps to prevent repeated tweaks of elements, which previous iterations have already addressed. When making a change, be sure to note:

- Why was the element updated?
- What problem is the update attempting to solve?
- What's improved about it?

In addition to keeping your team apprised of changes, it's useful to appoint a person (or a rotation of people) who can answer questions about the design system, or make updates to code, files, and documentation as needed. GitHub again has an answer for this with their 'office hours' system, as well as what they call 'First Responders':

> *"Most teams at GitHub have an on-call duty rotation that we call First Responder. Whoever is on call is responsible for triaging issues (assign degrees of urgency) and responding to requests for help or code review. Having someone on call means the rest of the team can stay focused on deep work. In addition to First Responder, we started*

doing office hours 3 days per week to give people a regular time to ask us questions in person. This is used for pairing on code, talking through product updates that need our support, and responding to general questions."

Whether you appoint 'first responders', set up office hours, or use a Slack channel to field requests and address issues, it's vital to the longevity and health of your design system that you keep the whole team in the loop and engaged with the system's evolution.

Guardians, ambassadors, and leaders

Process, responsibility, and accountability are hard to maintain in large organisations. It's even harder when you have more than one product team working with a design system, or when teams are based in different locations.

We're human. We forget things from time-to-time. Things slip through the cracks. And then — to put it bluntly — you have some people who resist adopting the system, for whatever reason.

You need someone — or a team of people — responsible for making sure the design system is adopted and maintained, and that all stakeholders are suitably educated and involved. This doesn't mean you have to adopt an overlord mentality; just that you need to be *realistic* about the system's chances of running smoothly — and evolving — without some level of oversight and management.

Design systems require leadership — whether it comes from a concerted, collective effort by designers at your company, a dedicated design systems team, and/or a 'design system lead'.

And keep-in-mind: the goal is to educate, not enforce. People don't generally respond well to orders. Approach the management of a design system from a teaching and collaborating perspective, not as the ruling authority.

With that said, let's look at a few different strategies for establishing design system leadership on your team.

You need to be realistic about the design system's chances of running smoothly, and evolving, without some level of oversight and management.

Appoint a design system lead

A design system lead's key responsibilities are to:

- Advocate for the system.
- Establish design system processes.
- Ensure that any processes for updates and maintenance are upheld.
- Educate designers on system design best practices.
- Research and discover new and improved ways to manage and maintain the system — whether it's technology, processes, or design tools that could help the team.
- Promote and seek opportunities for designers and developers to work together.
- Keep everyone up-to-date and engaged with the system.
- Deal with any resistance to the system.
- If applicable, recruit design system specialists to the team.

Appointing a 'design system lead' can help to keep things running smoothly. They advocate (and, when necessary, go to battle) for the system so your team (and design system) can thrive.

Form a design systems team

A dedicated design systems team has the advantage of being freed from business-as-usual tasks and product roadmaps, and instead can focus their time on design system tasks. These teams are generally staffed with people who have a broad set of skills, potentially including designer-developer hybrids, front-end engineers, and even roles like copywriters and animation specialists. These teams work on creating design system library assets, documentation, pattern libraries, and even specialist tools that facilitate the work of product teams.

Where designers on product teams can have a narrow vision of design at their company (i.e. they generally only see what their team works on — they don't see what every team is working on), the design systems team should have greater oversight of design across all product teams. This awareness helps to identify patterns and components that can be shared across teams — avoiding teams overlapping and needlessly creating the same elements twice.

11.14 link.medium.com/e6xYd06HGX

11.15 benlister.net

Ambassadors and guardians

For organisations with multiple product teams and/or locations, it's somewhat unrealistic to expect a single design system lead — or even a design systems team — to manage everything. They can't be everywhere at once. And perhaps most importantly, they can't be expected to know all the intricacies and edge cases of each product team's work, and the user and business problems they are solving (which is vital knowledge for creating things like design system patterns).

Appointing a design system ambassador on each product team alleviates some of this pressure, ensuring every team has a design system voice and guardian present in design critiques, sprints, and product discussions. These ambassadors report back to the design system team — or lead — creating a valuable feedback loop, and facilitating well-informed decisions.

Sprout Social (11.14) have successfully adopted this ambassador approach:

> *"Our design system ambassadors are designers from across the organization that act as liaisons between their embedded teams and the design systems team. They are our eyes, ears, and voice across the company. Design system ambassadors not only define and document their team's design patterns and components, but they also take ownership of them, keep their team synced on design system initiatives, and uncover ways to include design system work on their team's roadmaps."*

Sprout Social's Design Systems Team Lead, Ben Lister (11.15) continues:

> *"When looking for ambassadors, we seek out people who are not only passionate about design systems but also those who are systems thinkers, willing to stand up for good design and advocate for best practices."*

The great thing about this approach is — even if you're not empowered to hire a design system lead or create a separate team — you can suggest that you or other members of your team take on a "design system guardian" role. As a guardian, you and system-minded designers from other product teams meet to collaborate on creating and maintaining your system.

Whatever approach you choose, be mindful that a design system is unlikely to take-off — or survive after the fact — without leadership. Be proactive in helping your team and design system thrive. You can create a team and appoint leaders at the outset of a design system project, or introduce them as the project matures and gains trust (and a budget).

Closing thoughts

A design system is a marathon, not a sprint. They're never finished. A good design system is flexible and open to change. You will grow and develop your foundations, components, and patterns as you learn more about your user's needs and behaviour, and as your brand and business evolve.

Ultimately, the goal is for design systems to become integral to how your company designs and builds products. To achieve this you need to approach system design not just from a technical stance, but also from a position of cooperation. Diplomacy and communication are as important as the pixels you craft and the code you write.

Linzi Berry (**11.16**), the Design Systems Lead at Lyft, wrote an excellent article (**11.17**) on approaching design systems in a human-centered way. To quote from her article:

> *"Systems design is not only scientific and meticulous, it's the mastery of interacting with people in a sensitive and effective way. The system is an internal tool and our coworkers are its users. They're human, just like us, and they want to do a good job. By empathizing, reassuring, educating, remaining flexible, sharing, communicating, and staying positive — we've overcome many hurdles and are excited to take on new challenges in the future."*

The designs we create can shape our world in positive ways. When we design systematically, we are able to efficiently create better experiences for our users — but design systems also empower us to work better together.

11.16 twitter.com/taptodismiss

11.17 medium.com/tap-to-dismiss/art-of-diplomacy-2ad1e2cac795

My hope is that by reading this book, you are inspired and empowered — not just to lay strong foundations for the work you do, but also for the relationships you build. Perhaps the most powerful advantage design systems have is that they allow us to create better work *together*.

I sincerely hope you enjoyed this book, and that it helps you and your team.

Good luck :)

ABOUT THE AUTHOR

— Andrew Couldwell

Andrew is a web designer and developer, born and raised in Yorkshire, in the North of England. He started building websites in 2001, back when websites were made of table-based HTML and Flash movies.

He started his career at various agencies, where he was employed as a web developer, a web designer, and a product designer, respectively. Frustrated by the limited scope and challenges of the agency world, he left to pursue a new life of remote working from Cornwall, Spain, and London. During this period he did freelance design and web development for brands like NASA, Red Bull, MTV, Nike, Harvey Nichols, and Foursquare.

When not working on client projects, Andrew focusses on his long-time passion project: a website called Club of the Waves **(01)**. First launched in 2006, the site is an international showcase of artists and photographers whose work focusses on surfing and surf culture.

In 2014, he moved overseas to New York City to be the lead product designer of a new Adobe product. Working with a team of developers at Behance, together they launched Adobe Portfolio, a tool that helps creatives share their work online. In 2016, he moved onto a new challenge at WeWork as the system design lead, where he initiated, designed, and documented their digital brand guidelines, and two design systems.

In 2018, he returned to freelance design and development, working remotely for clients all around the world.

Andrew does his best work when he's designing impactful, meaningful digital products, and working with creative people who want to help people and make the world a better place. He also loves to build what he designs.

Currently based in Los Angeles, California, Andrew lives with his wife, Meagan, and their three cats. And they're expecting ~~their first child~~ twins in 2020!

See Andrew's portfolio at **roomfive.net**

Say hello @**andrewcouldwell**

01 clubofthewaves.com

Owl Studios

This book is a product of Owl Studios, who are a small but dedicated design and development studio. It was written and designed by Andrew Couldwell, and edited by Meagan Fisher.

We're wise — and often nocturnal — designers who code; together we have over 30 years of practice creating web experiences. We take on projects of all sizes, from web design and build, to product, branding, and system design. We also travel to do workshops and talk at design events, internationally.

If you want to work with us; reach out and say hello! We're excited to hear about your awesome project.

owlstudios.co

hello@owlstudios.co

Club of the Waves

This name appears a few times thoroughout this book — partly because it's a website driven by a design system, and partly because it's something I'm proud to share. Club of the Waves is a labour of love I founded back in 2006. It's an international showcase of artists and photographers whose work focusses on surfing and surf culture. Check out the website and find new artists and photographers I think you'll love.

clubofthewaves.com

@clubofthewaves

Acknowledgments

I couldn't have created this book without the support and love of my wonderful wife and best friend, Meagan Couldwell (**02**). Writing and publishing a book was only ever going to cost money, not make money. I had to take time out of paid work to do it. She only ever encouraged me to do this, and that's pretty amazing! Meagan also did a brilliant job editing this book — it simply wouldn't be what it is without her. Her patience, input, revisions, and contributions (as a web designer herself) made the content so much better — all for which I'm very grateful.

Also, thanks to our little family of cats! Fluffy, Theo, and Junior. I most certainly wrote some of this book with Fluffy on my lap, Theo pressed into me by my side, or attempting to type while Junior, Fluffy, or Theo tried to sit on the keyboard. Our little family of cats and my wife make me a happier person. A happy, healthy mind helps you do your best work.

I'd like to thank my amazing family: Mum, Ian, grandparents, uncles, aunties, cousins... everyone. Though I may live on a different continent to them now, they shaped who I am — and have always been supportive in my crazy endeavours to live and work abroad. And thank you to my 'new' family in the United States who have made me feel so welcome. I love you all.

Thanks to all my friends, internationally. Once upon a time, I virtually lived to work. It got me a long way in my career, but it never made me happy. One of the most important lessons I've learned is to strike a good work/life balance. The friends I've made along the way, in Yorkshire, Cornwall, London, and New York have made me a happier, healthier, and stronger person. *Though my liver might not share the same view!*

Professionally, almost everyone I've worked with has in some small or large way informed much of what I cover in this book. Good and bad, thank you for the learning experiences.

I'd like to specifically thank a few former work colleagues. Nick Stamas (**03**) is one of the rare people I've worked with whose talent and experimental nature pushed me to be better, learn, and grow. Working with Nick on design systems informed a good deal of the content of this book — and for that, he deserves huge credit and thanks. Also, thanks to Keaton Price (**04**), who's patient, systematic, and iterative approach to design problems *(and office politics)* is inspiring — and something I held in mind a good few times while writing this book. And finally, Bobby Ghoshal (**05**), who set me on the path to discovering the Foundations Model and the idea of Digital Foundations. He didn't tell me what to do or how to do it. Instead, he freed me from the chains of my daily routine and encouraged me to do what would ultimately be some of my best and most influential work to date.

I'd like to thank Shane Mielke (06). The only part of this book process I knew how to do was write. The rest was a mystery to me. Shane shared with me his story of how he self-published his book, *Launch It*, and everything he'd learned doing it.

Thank you to my good friend, Paul Davies (07). Paul took a chance on me early in my career, which proved to be a big turning point for me (08). 11 years later, he kindly volunteered to proof-read this book, which I graciously accepted. *It's just a shame he hated it! Only joking* :)

And finally, thank you! It means a lot to me that you read my book. I hope you enjoyed it and found it useful. If you did, I'd really appreciate it if you'd recommend this book to your friends, colleagues, and followers.

If I forgot you, I'm sorry, and thank you :)

02 owltastic.com

03 nickstamas.com

04 keaton.design

05 twitter.com/ghoshal

06 shanemielke.com

07 bhvr.co.uk

08 medium.com/@andrewcouldwell/i-nearly-quit-42c246c15b74

For you, Dad

I would like to dedicate this book to my dad, Michael Couldwell. I lost my dad to a short battle with cancer before my 30th birthday. It knocked me sideways. He raised me to be competitive — for better or for worse. Much of my teen years and young adulthood were spent trying to make my Dad proud. He never saw me leave England's shores to live and work in New York City. He only caught a glimpse of my career taking off before that. He never got to meet my wife, or my future kids. I often wonder how he'd feel about much of what I've done since he left. I wrote a book! I'm proud of that. I think he would be too.

So this book's for him. I love you, Dad.

FIN

CPSIA information can be obtained
at www.ICGtesting.com
Printed in the USA
LVHW071507140422
715916LV00007B/5

9 780578 540030